I0070023

Oonagh Monahan's 3rd edition of **MONEY FOR JAM** is a must-read for aspiring food entrepreneurs. Packed with practical advice and insider tips, this book is your essential guide to turning your passion for food into a successful business. A game-changer in the world of food entrepreneurship!

**Chef Brian McDermott**

A must read for anyone about to start their own food business. Everything you need to know in one place. Oonagh cuts through the noise and holds your hand on this exciting but daunting journey into life as a food producer.

**Jane Chambers, Shells Café, Sligo**

We've known Oonagh since she first mentored us in 2012, when Mescan Brewery was still just an idea. She has a tremendous knowledge of, and passion for, all things food. **MONEY FOR JAM** is a valuable resource for anyone starting a small food business and is packed full of useful information presented in a very accessible format.

**Cillian Ó Móráin, Mescan Brewery**

**MONEY FOR JAM** 1st edition absolutely changed my perspective about starting up a business. Full of wealth of knowledge and experiences from the first chapter to the very last. "Start where you are" is a business nugget I still hold on to; it gave me the push most needed to start my food business from our home kitchen. **MONEY FOR JAM** - a must-read for individuals with business ideas.

**Funké Egberongbe, FUNKÉ- Afro Caribbean Restaurant**

Oonagh has a wealth of knowledge about the Irish small food and drink business sector, if you are thinking of starting a food business, you will save yourself a lot of time and money reading this book!

**Aisling Flanagan, Rockfield Dairy/Velvet Cloud**

Oonagh's knowledge of the food business is second to none, enabling us to convert our food vision into a tangible food brand with a clear vision and focus for the future. A must read for anyone starting a food business.

**Dave and Áine Mullan, Fish & Bean Seafood Restaurant**

Oonagh Monahan is a font of knowledge, sound knowledge. There is something in this publication for everyone. For sure!

**Shane Smith, *YesChef Ireland*, "the magazine for lovers of good food"**

Oonagh is a recognised authority on starting a small food business. She is a highly experienced consultant and mentor, offering practical advice that draws on an experience base from working with hundreds of food businesses over many years. She has literally written the book and is highly knowledgeable on areas as diverse as food hygiene, product development, routes to market and on the many sources of help to someone starting out.

**John Magee, Head of Enterprise, LEO Mayo**

*MONEY FOR JAM* is the perfect start point for anyone thinking of starting a food business. It's full of tips and vital information that every small food business will need to get off the ground. It was a real help to me both starting and growing Noo Chocolates, and I recommend it as essential reading for every food business.

**Mary Corrigan, Noo Chocolates**

*MONEY FOR JAM* by Oonagh Monahan is an indispensable guide for aspiring food entrepreneurs. It is a treasure trove of practical wisdom and insider insights. Drawing from Oonagh's extensive experience in the Irish food industry this book is a 'must-have' resource for anyone looking to turn their passion for food into a thriving business in Ireland from concept to execution.

**Susan McLaughlin, Love A Little Sauces**

Anytime I met Oonagh, I learnt something new and beneficial. Her knowledge and passion about start-up food businesses was pivotal to our success. She illuminated pathways clearly and simply that helped our business grow.

**Redmond Cabot, Cabot's of Westport**

Oonagh is highly regarded as the 'go-to' professional for advice on turning bright food ideas into a viable business. Her help in bringing structure to our Research & Development has been invaluable – after all, even the wildest ideas can benefit from a bit of taming and organisation.

**Michael Liddle, Operations Director (New Projects), McCaughey Foods**

From my first year in start-up right through to ongoing product and branding development, *MONEY FOR JAM* has been my go-to source for guidance

**Fionntán Gogarty, Wildwood Balsamics**

# *More* MONEY FOR JAM

## The Essential Guide to Starting Your Own Small Food Business in Ireland, Northern Ireland or Great Britain

### THIRD EDITION

## Oonagh Monahan

·OAK·TREE·PRESS·

Published by OAK TREE PRESS, Cork T12 XY2N, Ireland
www.oaktreepress.com / www.SuccessStore.com

© 2024 Oonagh Monahan

First edition published 2013; Second edition 2017; this third edition 2024

A catalogue record of this book is available from the British Library.

ISBN 978 1 78119 586 4 (paperback)
ISBN 978 1 78119 587 1 (PDF)
ISBN 978 1 78119 588 8 (ePub)
ISBN 978 1 78119 589 5 (Kindle)

Cover design: Kieran O'Connor Design
Cover illustration: lepas2004 / iStockPhoto.com

Author photo: Kathy Burke Photography

All rights reserved. No part of this publication may be reproduced or transmitted in any form or by any means, including photocopying and recording, without written permission of the publisher. Such written permission must also be obtained before any part of this publication is stored in a retrieval system of any nature. Requests for permission should be directed to Oak Tree Press at info@oaktreepress.com.

Although the author and publisher have taken every care to ensure that the information published in this book is correct at the time of going to press, neither can take any responsibility for any loss or damage caused to any person as a result of acting on, or refraining from acting on, any information published herein. Professional advice should be obtained before entering into any legally binding commitments. No recommendation or endorsement is made or implied by the inclusion of any organisation in this book.

# CONTENTS

# CASE STUDIES

# ACKNOWLEDGEMENTS

It's hard to believe that it has been over 10 years since the first edition of *MONEY FOR JAM* was published. In that time, there have been many changes in the world, not least in the world of food and drink. Legislation continues to be amended, new legislation introduced, even more new food trends have emerged – especially in sustainable packaging and plant-based foods, many more new food businesses have been established, and unfortunately some have closed. Agriculture and food production methods continue to evolve too with the growth of organic farming and regenerative agriculture. The impact of Brexit, the Covid-19 pandemic and ingredient shortages have all impacted, and continue to impact on the food supply chain and on the ability of businesses to compete.

The reaction to the first and second editions of the book was really positive and encouraging. Nascent and start-up food producers, as well as established producers, have contacted me to say how helpful it has been to them, whether starting from scratch, growing their food businesses or developing new food products.

Now retitled *More MONEY FOR JAM*, all chapters in this third edition have been updated. I have continued to gather information from a variety of sources for this new edition. At the time of writing, many EU rules continue to apply in the UK and Northern Ireland as they have not yet written their own legislation post-Brexit. However, many of the same principles are likely to continue to apply, even if the detail of the legislation diverges. Nonetheless, for clarity, I have separated out information for food producers in Northern Ireland, Scotland, Wales and England in a new chapter (**Chapter 16**).

I have also added new case studies with examples of producers who do some things really well! Thanks again to the producers who have allowed me to feature them again in this edition, and also to all the new entrants. Contact details for all the producers featured in the case studies throughout the book can be found in **Chapter 17**. It's always a pleasure meeting and working with food producers who work so hard and have such passion for the food business and such a shame when they have to close, whatever the reason may be – as has happened to some of the producers included in case studies in the second edition.

Thank you so much to everyone who contributed in any way, to the producers who agreed to be featured, to the retailers for providing information, and to everyone who offered support and advice.

Finally, once again, thank you so much to my family, colleagues and friends for their patience and encouragement.

**Alpha Omega Consultants**
**Dromahair, Co. Leitrim, Ireland**
*June 2024*

# 1
# THE OPPORTUNITY

If you have ever thought about trying to earn some money from producing food, if you're the person everyone goes to for their lemon meringue pies, apple tarts and other desserts for family occasions, celebrations or other events; if you have a garden full of rhubarb or other fruit and make jam every year and give it away when you could be selling it; if you fancy the idea of making cheese or yogurt or ice cream or chocolate; or you are big into baking sourdough bread or making fermented foods or protein bites and would like to turn your hobby into a business but don't know where to start, then this is the book for you!

*More* MONEY FOR JAM is structured and written in an easy-to-follow and easy-to-read format. It tells you everything you need to know or shows you where to find it for yourself. It is not a textbook – think of it instead as your trusty companion, more of a handbook or manual. It aims to reassure both prospective and early-stage food producers and help them and existing producers to grow a sustainable business.

Don't be intimidated! *More* MONEY FOR JAM contains everything that someone who is new to the business of food needs to get started and to keep going. It will also help established producers to develop new products in a managed way, giving them the best chance of success with the least cost of time and money.

It covers the what, where, who and how for food producers – including legislation and registration, labelling and packaging, suppliers and distribution, marketing and sales. The complaint I hear all the time is that people don't even know where to start or who to ask for information in relation to starting a food business. Many are afraid to stick their heads above the parapet by asking the relevant state agencies such as the Environmental Health Officers (EHOs) at the Health Service Executive (HSE) in the Republic of Ireland or their local Council in Northern Ireland and the UK, the Department of Agriculture, Food & the Marine (DAFM), the Department of Agriculture, the Environment & Rural Affairs (DAERA) in Northern Ireland, the Food Safety Authority of Ireland (FSAI), the Food Standards Agency (FSA) for England, Wales & Northern Ireland, Food Standards Scotland (FSS), Bord Bia (the Irish Food Board) and so on. There is a common perception that doing so may bring unwanted attention – or worse, inspection! But you should know that the various agencies are there both to protect the consumer and to help you as a producer.

## Recent Trends

Keeping an eye on consumer trends is essential if you're thinking of starting up a new food business or developing new foods in an existing business. Look at the growth in popularity in recent years of fermented foods – kimchi or sourdough bread, for example – both now mainstream, as are high protein foods, which were aimed at sports people initially but are increasingly found in many people's shopping baskets. The growth of plant-based/vegan foods continues, as many consumers seek to reduce their meat intake for either health or environmental reasons, and other consumers are looking for protein alternatives.

The prevention, or at least the reduction, of food waste also is increasingly important and some new foods on the market include those made using spent grains from the brewing industry – value is added to turn them into a consumer food instead of being sold as low-value animal feed.

Sustainability has grown in importance, and we will take a look at that both in terms of environmental impact and the financial or commercial sustainability of your business.

Simplicity, wholesomeness, health, convenience and good nutritional credentials, along with ethics, quality, craft, provenance and heritage, are still important considerations as consumers continue to increase their awareness and knowledge about the foods they eat.

Shoppers are really interested in knowing where the food products they purchase are made and who made them. There is a huge choice of foods available now, whether home-produced or imported, so the decision to buy a food more often than not will depend on whether that particular food addresses these concerns. The major retailers have latched on to this and promote local producers on their own-brand foods and in their stores - they know it's good for business.

Many smaller shops have responded well to this demand for quality and choice from customers. A typical example is a small butcher in a country town, who might have sold bags of potatoes and some vegetables, might have had packets of spices on the counter, even might have offered the occasional home-baked apple tart. The same butcher has now re-branded from, say, 'Quinn's Butchers' to 'Quinn's Fine Foods & Delicatessen'. The shop has had a facelift, it's more attractive inside and the layout has been tidied up. It is still selling the same foods but it has raised the bar in terms of how the consumer sees it. As a result, it is attracting new customers, offering an outlet for and showing support to local producers, and embracing the local food culture that has continued to grow in recent years.

The continued growth in numbers of other nationalities moving into Ireland and the UK has brought more food varieties and a diverse food culture with it, and consumers have lots of opportunities to try out new foods. In fact, foods many of us consider to be part of our basic shopping basket today were considered exotic and unusual years ago. The same thing will happen in the future for foods that are considered exotic or unusual now and we look forward to that with anticipation!

## Opportunities for Small Food Producers

So what does all this mean for you, the would-be food producer? Let's say you have been baking or fermenting or making jam or chocolate or protein snacks at home just for family and friends or for local fundraisers. Perhaps you have decided that you would like to make some money out of it either to add to the household income or with the ambition to grow it into a decent business that will earn you a living, maybe even leave the job you're in and chase your dream of being a successful food producer! If so, then you need to know what you have to do to turn that hobby into a proper business.

Many consumers want to see money staying in the country, preferably locally. So, locally-made produce is very much welcomed and can be seen in shops everywhere. The adage "If you can see it, you can be it" applies – the more local producers there are in shops, the more that encourages others.

Consumers like the idea of artisan or home-made foods. You might portray the image of a country kitchen making scones and jam in a cottage with roses around the door, while all the time you're really in a state-of-the-art food production unit in your converted garage! While the reality might be less romantic as you outgrow your kitchen or small premises, it is important to maintain that brand image for your customers, if that's what they are looking for. We will look at branding in **Chapter 6**.

Irish and British consumers are more discerning now than they used to be. They are used to having a wide selection of foods to choose from, they expect good quality, and they are used to paying a little more for it. Farmers' and Country markets and small speciality retailers are the norm for many shoppers, not just some quaint novelty. Consumers will still make a special trip for special purchases that they cannot get in supermarkets.

## The Food Market

Artisan/speciality food production in Ireland and Britain is made up of a large number of small food producers, making niche products, generally in small batches, using artisan techniques. The most recent CSO figures (www.cso.ie/en/releasesandpublications/fp/pfavca/foodandagricultureavaluechainanalysis/householdconsumption/) show 1,352 domestically-owned food and drink producers in Ireland, who made €9.8 billion worth of foods. Most of this production is in the dairy and meat sectors (mostly large producers). In the same year, household/personal consumption of food and drink (including imported food) was €10.5 billion. Of this, €1.2 billion was spent on tea, coffee, readymade foods and processed snacks. So the market potential for a new entrant is significant, although also very competitive.

The artisan/speciality food and drinks sector continues to grow in the UK also, where there are over 6,000 small producers, clearly making it a very important part of the food industry and of the economy there (**Chapter 16**).

The key point is that, if your products are of good quality, with a strong provenance, are consistent, have great taste and flavour and ideally provide something a little different, then there is probably a market for them.

## What Does 'Artisan' or 'Traditional' or 'Farmhouse' Mean?

Descriptions including 'fresh', 'natural', 'artisan', 'farmhouse' and so on are used widely, and may not always be accurate. Over-use of these words in describing foods has confused consumers and diluted their true meaning.

For the consumer, the word 'artisan' or 'farmhouse' usually means a connection to the individual who makes the food. In the consumer's mind, this means literally home-made or hand-made. Both the FSAI (Ireland) and FSA (UK) have published some guidance on this, which you can find on their websites. For example, to be 'artisan', you must employ fewer than 10 people (including yourself) and produce less than 1,000 litres or kg per week, among other considerations.

Consumers expect 'artisan' to mean superior taste, flavour, handmade, small-scale, with a direct connection to the producer, high standards – and so … more expensive? While consumers like the idea that someone has made this food themselves, that it's not from some big, faceless, corporate, automated process, the question is whether they are willing to pay for it? The difficulty faced by small food producers is that they are in competition with those very same big, faceless, corporate, automated processors and imports that have economies of scale, which means they can make and sell their foods much more cheaply. It's not so much that artisan or craft foods are expensive; it's that other foods, because of mass production, have become relatively cheap.

So, the artisan producer has a job to do in promoting all the qualities of their foods that justify the price – back to flavour, quality, provenance, authenticity, the person, home-made, farmhouse, local and so on. Those are your potential unique selling points (USPs) – more about them in **Chapter 2**. Underestimate their value or forget them at your peril!

## 'Local' Is Important

When you think about 'local', do you think about your corner shop, village, town, county, province or country? When is local not local?

For some people, local food means that it comes from a nearby farmer, butcher, baker or a neighbour, or certainly within a distance of 100 km according to guidelines. Consumers say that they like to support local producers and to shop locally, but if your name or the name of your food or business does not immediately tell the shopper where the food is from or that it's made locally, then you need to make sure that you let them know some other way. You can use your labels and branding to help communicate this message – more about that later in **Chapter 6**, when we look at branding and marketing.

If someone goes to the trouble to look for locally-made food, then they usually have a good reason to do so. Most of the time they want to be sure that their food can be traced back to where it was made. The phrase 'farm to fork' is used commonly now, and it's all about traceability and transparency – knowing where food and its ingredients come from and giving the consumer trust.

When is Irish not Irish? Or English/Scottish/Welsh, or not English/Scottish/Welsh for that matter? In many ways, it is just a matter of opinion. For example:

- If it's made in the country? Even if the company is not locally/domestically-owned?
- If it's not made in the country, but outsourced to a manufacturer in another country but the company is (for example) Irish-owned?
- If the basic ingredients are not grown in the country, yet the food is made here by an indigenous company, such as chocolate or coffee?
- If the name implies that it's indigenous?
- Or does it have to be 100% from the country (Ireland or England or wherever) – all the ingredients, ownership, etc.?

Whatever the answer, there is a great opportunity for you to shout about the fact that your foods are made locally, by you, in your kitchen/premises, employing local staff (even if it is just you and your family), and using as many local ingredients as possible ... or a combination of some or all of these.

## The Potential for Small Food Businesses

The small food business has potential for several reasons:

- Consumers expect to be offered a wide variety of new foods;
- Consumers are willing and able to discern and to pay for high-quality locally-produced food;
- Increased education and awareness levels among farmers and food and drink producers about consumer needs and wants;
- Increased popularity of locally-produced, artisan, home-made and farmhouse products;
- An image of a country that is an unspoilt tourist destination that is green, natural and wholesome;
- Availability of high-quality and high-profile local foods from well-known, local artisan food producers across the country, raising the profile for all producers;
- The use of local ingredients by chefs, who post about them in their social media;
- The availability of new routes to market (**Chapter 6**).

As far as the shopper and consumer are concerned, one of the main advantages is that there is a story behind the food that they can identify with (the 'provenance'), but most of all, that the food has superior quality and taste. It can have all the local, eco, history and whatever you're having yourself but, if it doesn't have great quality and taste, then no one will buy it again. This leads to a key point about developing your food idea – make sure you get the taste and quality right first before you start telling everyone how great it is!

Food producers and suppliers should never forget the value and importance of building their brand around the provenance of their produce. Consumers like the idea that the food they buy is artisan, home-made, almost as if it has been made for them especially. They like to hear about the producers themselves, the farm, the family, the recipe being handed down through generations, tradition, history of the herd or breed and so on. It helps the consumer to satisfy themselves that the food is local, has not been overly-processed and meets their expectations of taste and quality.

## Food Tourism

Food tourists are 'culinary tourists', who seek out unique, memorable eating and drinking experiences wherever they go. They want to try new foods and taste foods in their traditional context, foods associated with an area. In response to this demand, Visitor Experiences and Food Trails have increased significantly in numbers over the past five years (more in **Chapter 6**).

## Sustainability

This is certainly *the* buzz-word, or at least one of the buzzwords, of the past couple of years. Consumers say that they are concerned that the food they buy is locally-produced, that it is environmentally sustainable with low food miles as well as a low carbon footprint perhaps. What does all this mean exactly though? And how can a consumer be sure that the story they're hearing from the producer is honest and not just 'green-washing'? In other words, how can consumers be sure you're really doing what you say you're doing?

Environmental sustainability is important of course – most people realise that the work we do in our businesses should not impact negatively on the environment and ultimately on our planet. However, it's not just what you do, it is also important to be aware of what your suppliers are doing, as well as your distributors, and anyone else associated with your food business.

Here are a few simple steps that producers can take, that are not only good for the environment but often can save money too:

- Use renewable energy, whether from a supplier or by installing your own solar panels or windmill or heat pump;
- Change all your lightbulbs to LED;

- Install motion sensors so that lights go off when no one is in the room or corridor (though this might require some arm-waving if you're standing or sitting still for a while!);
- Monitor food waste, with the aim of preventing it or at least reducing it;
- Consider donating surplus food to organisations like FoodCloud (www.food.cloud) or FareShare (www.fareshare.org.uk); if you run a bakery, café or restaurant, sell off unsold foods at the end of the day through apps like Too Good To Go (next.toogoodtogo.com/en-ie/);
- Switch to electric vehicles – powered by your own solar electricity, perhaps;
- Actively promote reuse and recycling, both internally and among your suppliers and customers;
- Source consumable supplies that can be recycled/returned to the supplier for recycling – for example, printer cartridges, glass bottles and jars, shipping crates/boxes;
- Choose suppliers that adopt best environmental practices, where practical;
- Buy products and services that have the least environmental impact – including buying from local suppliers, where possible.

If you make a start working your way through these, then shout about it! Tell your customers, write an environmental policy and publish it, monitor your progress, then tell everyone about the progress you've made.

Hand-in-hand with this is financial or commercial sustainability. While many of the actions you take above will save you money, you need to continue to actively manage your money (see **Chapter 8**), keep an eye on your costs, your cash flow and your profits. Shop around when sourcing compostable/recyclable packaging for example. Keep an eye on Government grants that may be available.

In the long run, food and drink producers, indeed all businesses, cannot afford NOT to be environmentally sustainable. It's good for everyone, and it's good for business. You'll find information about agencies and supports to help your business become – and stay – sustainable in **Chapter 17**.

# 2
# DEVELOPING YOUR IDEA

## Where to Start?

How do you eat an elephant? One bite at a time.

First things first, then. Don't be paralysed by fear! Starting your own food production business is not like splitting the atom or finding the cure for a terminal disease. It's just food. Plenty of other people are already doing it, so it cannot be that difficult – can it?

It might not be rocket-science, but nonetheless, there are so many different things to consider when starting up a food business that it can seem overwhelming at first.

## What Will You Make?

Before you do anything else, you must make up your mind about what food you want to produce. Most small food producers get into the food business because they love making something in particular or they have a source of ingredients that they want to use, such as fruit, milk or seaweed. Others get into it because they see a business opportunity in a niche area. Many new producers try to do too many varieties too soon and become overwhelmed trying to manage them all. Some decide to produce foods that they really don't enjoy making but do so because they think there is a market. Others do not have the skills required to make the food they think they would like to sell.

It is best to go with your strengths. If you don't enjoy making it, you will not stick at it. So, the first thing is to remember is that you are now in business, selling food for money. It may be just a few jars, loaves or tarts to begin with, even in just one shop or market. Take baby steps, and when your confidence builds, then start to walk with your foods to a few more shops ... jump to shops in the next town ... run, grow the business if that's what you want to do, export even ... but all in good time.

New producers get all excited about their venture, which is great. I love the enthusiasm of start-ups. However, sometimes the excitement focuses on the fun stuff: branding, packaging design, thinking about growth in the future, nationwide sales ... before they ever develop their recipes and operations properly. So first, you have to make something – a bit of product development is needed.

## Where Do Ideas Come From?

For many people, getting into the small food business is a matter of looking differently at what they might be doing already. As I said above, you might make desserts on request for family and friends already and now want to sell them to the public, for money! Perhaps it's a case of trying a new venture simply because you've always wanted to give it a try. Or maybe you've lost your job (or your spouse/partner has) and it's a case of having to do something to bring in some money. Perhaps you've come into some money through redundancy and want to take the opportunity to give it a go while you can support yourself.

Whatever the reason for it, now you need to get your thinking cap on and decide what it is that you want to produce:

- **Have you spotted a gap in the market?** *I can't get good gluten-free, vegan snacks anywhere.*
- **What are you good at?** *People love my lemon meringue pie or Kombucha.*
- **Do you already have a source of ingredients?** *We have loads of blackcurrants in the garden ... I could make jam, pies, sauce!*
- **What are the market trends?** *People need something healthy to eat to give them energy when they're on the go/they want an indulgent treat/they are concerned about the planet/they need to increase their protein intake.*

## Who Are Your Customers?

You will need to consider who will buy and eat your wonderful food – this is called your 'target market'. Your potential customers fall into two groups – the general buying public (the consumer), which is usually referred to as B2C (Business to Consumer) and the retailers who will buy from you to sell on to *their* customers (B2B or Business to Business). Both groups look for the same things: quality, taste, value and something different or new.

Your target market is made up of consumers from various demographics. Think about who they may be: families, older people, children, single people, married couples, men, women, healthy eaters, fitness fanatics, dieters, indulgers, students, office- or home-workers. Your target market will influence the size of portion you make: large or small, multi-pack or single pack? Your portion size in turn will influence your selling price.

Next, consider your packaging: pre-packed or unwrapped? If your food is aimed at the eat-on-the-go market, then both portion size and packaging style both need to be considered. There is more detail about product development in **Chapter 5**.

Retailers are also your potential customers, otherwise you may not reach the consumer at all. Many retailers are keen to promote Irish producers: they see the sense in offering consumers a choice, and promoting local producers is a way of bringing in more trade. What you must remember, though, is that the retailer will not want more of the same – so try to offer something different to help them attract more shoppers.

## Who Are Your Competitors?

Every business and every product has a competitor, even if it not a direct competitor doing the same thing as you, or whether it is an obvious one or not. Realising and acknowledging that fact is really important when it comes to promoting and selling your food.

If you go into almost any small shop, there will be at least two varieties of most foods. Take apple tarts, for example – your competitor might be another home baker in the locality, or a large bakery delivering to the same shop, or the shop's own in-store bakery.

Most shopkeepers like to offer their customers a choice, so they provide a range for the shopper to choose from.

Direct competitors include anyone else making apple tarts. Indirect competitors, on the other hand, will be making rhubarb or other fruit tarts or desserts that might distract your potential buyer away from buying your apple tarts. In other words, your competitors include other small and local food producers, as well as the large-scale suppliers, imports, and alternatives.

You should benchmark yourself and your food against your competitors. What are they doing well that you might emulate or not bother trying? What can you do that is better than whatever is already out there for sale? What price are they selling at? What demographic are they targeting? What is their packaging like? Can you get a longer shelf life on your food?

## What Is a USP?

A Unique Selling Point (USP) is a characteristic or attribute that distinguishes your foods from your competitors. Identifying and promoting your food's USPs – it can have more than one (the more the merrier!) – is an on-going task. You can't just mention them once and sit back waiting for either the customers or the money (or both) to pour in! You will need to continue to develop USPs and to remind your customers about them all the time.

Some examples of a USP might include novel packaging, 'free-from', natural, no preservatives or additives, low fat or high protein, home-made, or homegrown ingredients. Is it locally-produced, using local ingredients, or organic, or is it a new type of food product, new to this country, new to this area, healthy, luxurious, in different portion sizes – it could be anything! Whatever your food's USPs are, you must take the time to write them down, and then be able to articulate them clearly and promote them all the time.

Your USPs define your food's competitive advantage. It is essential to identify what makes *Oonagh's Apple Pie* different from its many competitors, on as many different fronts as you can.

## Who Should You Talk to First?

If you go to the websites of the Food Safety Authority of Ireland (www.fsai.ie), the Food Standards Agency (www.food.gov.uk) or Food Standards Scotland (www.foodstandards.gov.scot), they will tell you that the first thing you should do is acquaint yourself with the relevant legislation. For most people, that's enough to send them running for the hills as it can be very intimidating.

However, if you're going to be in this food business game, then there is no avoiding the legislation. The important thing is to know what applies to you and what does not. There is the challenge – how do you find this out? And, once you know what applies to you, then how do you interpret it?

Depending on the foods you want to produce, then your kitchen might be either very straightforward to organise (bread, cakes, jam, dips) or might be more complicated (meat, dairy, prepared salads, large amounts of anything). If you are going to make anything at home, or even if you plan to convert your garage or move into a small premises, then the very first thing you must do is to phone your local Environmental Health Officer (EHO) – at the HSE in Ireland (www.hse.ie/eng/services/list/1/environ/opening-a-new-food-business/) or at your Council in Northern Ireland or the UK (register.food.gov.uk/new). These are the people who will give you approval for producing most foods. Microbreweries also must register with the EHOs.

If you are planning to get into hen or duck egg production, or animal slaughter or if you're handling and/or processing meat, or fish, or making dairy products, then in Ireland you need to contact either the Local Authority Veterinary Office (www.gov.ie/en/publication/942f74-local-authorities/), the local office of the Department of Agriculture (DAFM) (www.agriculture.gov.ie) or the Sea Fisheries Protection Authority (www.sfpa.ie). In Northern Ireland, contact the Department of Agriculture, Environment & Rural Affairs (DAERA) (www.daera-ni.gov.uk); in the UK, contact the Animal & Plant Health Agency (APHA) (apha.gov.uk). The local Councils in Ireland and the UK also may inspect establishments involved in animal slaughter and handling and/or processing meat. So, check out their website or just call them to find out who you need to talk to.

If you don't know who to call, just call any one of them and they'll point you in the right direction. We will look in more detail in **Chapter 4** at food safety and hygiene.

## Getting Organised

For the best chances of success, you will need to think through all of the issues that affect how you will make, where you will make and how you will package and label your food. In addition to your job as production manager, initially you also most likely will be the financial controller, sales and marketing manager, office manager and administrator, trainer, staff supervisor (if you have anyone working with you), delivery van driver, and chief bottle washer!

It is very difficult keeping on top of everything, of that there is no doubt. Your chances of success will improve if you at least know all the things you are supposed to remember. Make a list and write it down (keeping everything in your head is impossible and only gives you one more thing to try to remember!) and, if you can't do it all yourself, then get some help. There is a useful Action Plan (if I may say so myself!) that you can download from my website (www.alphaomega.ie/shop) to help you identify and remember everything you need to do. And because you have kindly bought this book, the code for your free download is M4J3ACTION.

Many people who have started up a small food business from home may have to or at least try to maintain their 'other' jobs as housekeeper, parent, cleaner, cook, doctor, sports coach and taxi-driver. In my experience, women are particularly guilty of this. You need to acknowledge the fact that you have now set up a business. It might be at home – but it is still a business. Schedule time for when you will be 'at work' and, during that time, no other household chores should distract you. Easier said than done, I know, but time management is essential and you must aspire to achieving that goal ultimately. If you cannot get help, then accept the fact that it will take you longer to get your new business off the ground as you simply won't have enough time to devote to it.

## Common Reasons for Failure ... and How to Avoid Them!

Something like 90% of all new food products fail, and usually for one or more of these reasons:

- **Poor market research among consumers or retailers or poor market orientation (in other words, trying to sell to the wrong people):** You thought your food was great, your family and friends agreed with you, but none of the customers you tried to sell it to wanted it. So maybe you weren't targeting the right customers, or the right shops, or in the right locality, or perhaps there is already a well-established or even a better or cheaper version already on the market and it is proving very difficult to convert shoppers to buy yours. People can be slow to change their shopping habits;

- **Technical or production problems:** Making a few cakes in your kitchen might have been manageable, but once you start making 100 every week, you might find that it just cannot be done at home due to limitations with your mixer, oven, and/or refrigerator. Or, while your recipe worked well for a 6" cake, it didn't rise when you tried to scale it up for a 12" cake. In this case, you needed to do some recipe and method trials and tweaking (product development, in other words – see **Chapter 5**);

- **Insufficient marketing effort:** One of the jobs that some food producers hate most is having to get out there and tell people about their food. Promoting it, talking about it and posting regularly on social media are activities that are essential but many producers feel uncomfortable or lack confidence in doing. Most will be happiest in the kitchen, up to their arms in flour or sauce. However, if you won't or can't do it yourself, then get someone who will and who will do a good job representing you and your foods and will make sales. We will look at how best to approach this in **Chapter 6**;

- **Bad timing:** Nothing as obvious as trying to sell Christmas cakes in July, but perhaps the market wasn't ready for your chilli chocolate bars/low calorie stout/banana protein cake. Indeed, it may have been something you could not have anticipated, such as a local factory closing down with job losses, or cost of living increases, the result being that people are not willing to spend money on perceived indulgences or foods that may not be as cheap as mass-produced varieties;

- **Higher costs than anticipated:** If sales and marketing is one bugbear, then financial planning and costs analysis is the other for most food producers. Nearly everyone hates looking at the figures but you absolutely must calculate how much it costs you to make, pack, distribute and sell the food. You should do this sooner rather than later. If you don't do it, then you cannot know how much to charge your B2B customers or put a retail price on your foods for your B2C customers, except by taking a wild guess. If, at the end of the year, you have worked every hour of every day and sold hundreds of pots or pies but still have no money for shoes or a holiday, or worse, cannot pay the bills, then there is a problem. We will look at how best to approach this in **Chapter 8**.

In order to increase your chances of success, learn from the experience of others:

- If you cannot create demand for a brand new product, then produce to known consumer demand for your target market;
- Get the training or help you need – don't presume you know it all or have to do it all;
- Don't ignore any tasks that you don't like!
- Develop a website/online sales for foods that can be shipped easily. You'll need help/resources for this;
- Articulate your USPs and brand values clearly – quality, flavour, taste, provenance;
- Build awareness about your brand and your foods by telling people about them all the time – word of mouth, advertising, competitions, promotions, sponsorships, networking;
- Use your network of friends, neighbours, family and colleagues – it's great for spreading the word and for exchanging information;
- Develop new markets over time – always be on the lookout for opportunities, don't get complacent, you never know who will come in on your turf;

- Use and put the effort into the right social media channels for your target demographic;
- Update your product range and keep it fresh by bringing out seasonal and occasional varieties, or by trying new packaging and labels.

In order to maximise your chances of success, control the things you can control. Find out the things you don't know, don't ignore them. Knowledge is power. After that, you are at the mercy of the marketplace, the economy, and the unknown unknowns!

## Just Do It!

If you're not already paralysed by fear, then you might be overwhelmed at the thought of trying to manage everything. While sometimes ignorance can be bliss, this is not a strategy I recommend! Most producers don't go from start-up to huge volumes overnight. It is most likely that your success will grow slowly at a steady pace.

There is a bigger danger that you might plan and plan and plan, but never actually make anything. My advice is Just Do It!

Get on with it! Make a couple of loaves/pots/jars/bags and get yourself down to your corner shop and see whether they'll take them from you for re-sale. What's the worst that can happen?

# 3

# NAVIGATING FOOD SAFETY & HYGIENE LEGISLATION

Before you even begin to tackle food safety and food hygiene legislation, remember that a lot of it is common sense, just scaled-up. First, let's take a look at who is responsible for food legislation and for monitoring that it's being done correctly.

The concern that people most often voice to me is that they are afraid that the authorities will either stop them from starting up at all or close them down and prevent them continuing. There is only one answer to that – you must make sure you keep your Environmental Health Officer (EHO) or Local Authority/Council or DAFM Inspector (if you are farm based) on-side!

The key to this is communication, so contact them sooner rather than later. They will visit your home kitchen or small unit and take a look at your set-up. They will tell you whether it is suitable or not (and you may be surprised to find that you have little or no work to do to get it up to scratch!). They will offer you great advice about what changes you might have to make.

Your EHO or Inspector is your best advisor – these are the people you must satisfy. And if you don't register with them (in other words, let them know you're in business), they will catch up with you eventually. Whether it's from spotting your foods for sale in shops, at markets or shows, seeing your adverts or just hearing about you, they will find you!

While all of this might sound a little frightening, be assured that the FSAI, FSA, DAFM, DAERA, EHO or Council Food Inspectors are there to help you. So, who are they?

## Competent Authorities

The legislation mentions 'competent authorities' a lot. These are the government agencies and departments that are responsible for writing and enforcing the food legislation. So, who are they?

In the Republic of Ireland, the competent authorities are:

- Department of Agriculture, Food & the Marine (DAFM) – www.gov.ie/en/organisation/department-of-agriculture-food-and-the-marine/;
- Food Safety Authority of Ireland (FSAI) – www.fsai.ie;
- Health Services Executive/Environmental Health Officers (HSE/EHO) – you can register on-line at www.hse.ie/eng/services/list/1/environ/opening-a-new-food-business/ (though sometimes a phone call might be more helpful in developing a relationship with your EHO);
- Local Authority Veterinary Inspector – www.gov.ie/en/publication/942f74-local-authorities;
- Sea-Fisheries Protection Authority (SFPA) – www.sfpa.ie.

For more information, go to www.fsai.ie/business-advice/starting-a-food-business/competent-authorities/.

In the UK, the competent authorities are:

- Food Standards Agency (FSA) for Northern Ireland, England and Wales – www.food.gov.uk;
- Food Standards Scotland – www.foodstandards.gov.scot;
- Marine Scotland (for aquaculture) – www.marine.gov.scot.

The Food Safety Authority of Ireland (FSAI) is the government appointed authority dedicated to protecting public health and consumer interests in the area of food safety and hygiene. Its principal function is to take all reasonable steps to ensure that food produced, distributed or marketed in Ireland meets the highest standards of food safety and hygiene reasonably available and to ensure that food complies with legal requirements or, where appropriate, with recognised codes of good practice.

The FSAI is responsible for the enforcement of all food legislation in Ireland. It does this through the EHOs at the HSE, DAFM, County and City Councils, SFPA and other bodies. Which of these applies to you and your food business depends entirely on what you are making:

- For most people producing small quantities of food at home, it's the EHOs. The EHOs' job is to ensure that food legislation is followed properly. They are also educators and advisors and they work very closely with the owners of food businesses to build compliance with the law. The EHO ensures that you, as a food producer, understand that there is a law, what your obligations are under that law and what the possible consequences might be if you do not comply;

- DAFM is responsible for anyone producing eggs, processing milk or making dairy products. Anyone who wishes to manufacture a dairy product or process milk for direct human consumption must contact the Dairy Hygiene Division within DAFM in the first instance. An information pack is issued to the potential producer, outlining what is involved and covering requirements for both raw and pasteurised cows' milk, goats' milk, and sheep's milk.

FSAI's website (www.fsai.ie) publishes for sale a *Safe Catering Pack*, with a DVD, which has all the documentation you need. You can also download the records forms free from the website.

In the UK, the Food Standards Agency (FSA) is an independent non-ministerial Government Department. The EHOs are based in the Councils and so they are your first port of call if you are thinking about starting up a new food business – see www.food.gov.uk/businessindustry/hygieneratings/food-law-inspections. You can register your new business online at www.gov.uk/food-business-registration and arrange for the Council to visit you to inspect and approve your kitchen and premises. The FSA website (www.food.gov.uk/business-industry/startingup) has a useful checklist for starting up, helping you think about many business issues (some of these issues are useful for any business, not just food).

In Northern Ireland and the UK, you don't need to be inspected or approved if you sell directly to the public or to retailers like caterers, pubs and restaurants, as long as:

- Food is less than 25% of your trade;
- You don't handle any wild game meat products;
- You don't sell food outside the county in which your business is registered.

However, you must be inspected and approved by your local Council if your business involves handling meat, fish, egg or dairy products.

In Scotland, similar support is available from Food Standards Scotland (www.foodstandards.gov.scot).

## Is Your Kitchen Good Enough?

Most modern kitchens are well-equipped to provide all that is needed to satisfy the requirements for kitchen production – in other words, you can start straight away. But you need to ensure that what you are making will not possibly pose a health risk to anyone who eats it. You are selling to the public now, so what might be OK for you and your family at home might not be OK for food being sold to paying consumers.

Simple things like keeping everything really clean and tidy, not having family or pets running around, being organised, keeping your food business ingredients separate from your household ingredients and so on will go a long way to getting your kitchen in order. Separation of home and work ingredients can be achieved very simply by having a dedicated cupboard or shelf, buying some big lunchboxes and sticking a label on them so that other members of the household don't use them or mess with them. If you don't have a space (or money) for a second fridge, and your EHO or Inspector says it's OK to do so, put your refrigerated food business ingredients into separate, labelled containers – 'Hands Off: Dad's/Mum's work ingredients' (and keep reminding yourself and your family that you're in business now!).

You'll need separate sinks for washing your hands and for washing utensils. Many modern kitchens have a little side sink between the main sink and the draining board. There you go – two sinks – or perhaps you have a second sink in a utility room.

You can't have any laundry in your kitchen – that means no washing machine – it must be in the utility room.

A rumour that abounds is that you need everything tiled from floor to ceiling or else stainless steel everywhere. Not true! The legislation simply calls for all surfaces to be easily cleanable. In other words, smooth, non-porous, in good repair. If your kitchen counter is made from marble or Formica or similar, then that will be fine. If you have a wooden surface, then it shouldn't be deeply scored with knife marks as bacteria like the dirt that gets trapped in these, so the best thing is to use a plastic chopping board (although these can also get damaged by knives over time) or cover it with a plastic cloth if you're going to be working directly on it.

Best to remove all clutter from the area you're working in. If there are plants on the window sills, remove them while you're working in case they fall over and spill out onto your food or work surface.

If you are doing a lot of cooking that generates steam and condensation on your windows, you will need an extractor fan. Your hob or cooker hood might do the job. Your windows should be kept closed unless you're happy to put flyscreens on them.

Keep the dog, cat and children out while you're preparing food.

It's all pretty much common sense. The bottom line is that if you're not sure, ask your EHO or Inspector.

Finally, if your kitchen is approved but you find your oven is too small or your equipment is not suitable, then you might want to consider your options – see the next section. However, the solution might even be simpler than that – get up earlier in the morning. Seriously! One client of mine complained that her oven was too small and she couldn't supply to meet the demand. It turned out she only made one batch on a Sunday morning. Seems obvious I know, but sometimes even the obvious eludes us.

## What If Your Kitchen Isn't Good Enough?

If you can't use your kitchen at home for some reason, whether through your own choice or if you've been inspected and you've been told that it's not suitable legally, or if the changes you have to make to get it up to standard are too much for you to do, or it's too small for the volume you're making, then what are your options?

One baker that I know started off using the kitchen in a pub that wasn't in use. The kitchen was perfectly serviceable and, after a good cleaning and the 'go ahead' from the EHO, he was in business, and the pub-owner was delighted to get some rental income. Another producer started off using a closed-down fast food place to make sandwiches for distribution to local schools and businesses. Someone else I know used the kitchen in a small café that was only open during the summer season – she started off there in the winter, just to get going, and then moved into bigger premises when she was up and running and had proved there was a market for her food (the proof being the fact that it was selling), and since the café was due to reopen for the summer, she was on a deadline.

A number of food units have been built around the country that can be rented by the hour, week or longer term. In Ireland, Local Enterprise Offices (LEOs), Councils, the Rural Development Companies (or LEADER companies, as everyone still calls them) and some community and private enterprises have built proper food units finished to food production standard that you can rent – contact your local Council, Community Office or Enterprise Office/Company to enquire. There are several across the UK (try Google to find them). I have compiled a list that you can download free at www.alphaomega.ie/product/rent-kitchen-space/.

## Food Safety & Hygiene Legislation

Food safety and hygiene legislation is concerned about four issues:

- The protection of health;
- Making sure that proper information is given (so that the consumer is properly informed);
- The prevention of fraud (horsemeat, anyone?);
- Freedom of trade (throughout the EU).

The last one isn't really an immediate concern for you, day-to-day – nor, hopefully, the second last!

The legislation that applies generally to small food producers are *Regulations EC 178/2002* (which sets out the general requirements of food law and food safety), *EC 852/2004* (the hygiene of foodstuffs) and possibly *EC 853/2004* (specific hygiene rules for food of animal origin). There is also Irish legislation, *SI 369 of 2006*, which is mostly about your responsibility as a food producer to comply with the law and about enforcement of the legislation.

If you read all the legislation, you'll possibly find yourself a little bewildered. It's a really good idea to ask someone to help you with this. If you're feeling brave, download a copy of *EC 852/2004* from www.fsai.ie and jump to Annex II to start. Go back and read the rest of it when you have drawn breath.

All food service providers, caterers, supermarkets and retailers require their food producers, processors and suppliers to comply with food safety legislation. In order to make sure that you address the concerns of your customers, and because it's the law, then you, as a new producer, must comply with the relevant quality and food safety regulations, and what's more, to be seen to be in compliance. This goes whether you decide to sell through shops or direct to the customer from your back door or through farmers' or country markets.

A good reference document is the *Guide to Food Law for Artisan/Small Food Producers Starting a New Business* available for free download from www.fsai.ie, which will direct you to all the legislation you need. Since it's all EU legislation, the guide can be used by food businesses in any EU country.

## Jargon

You will find the definitions associated with food legislation in Article 2 of *EC 852/2004* and in Articles 2 and 3 of *EC 178/2002*. Here are a few:

- **'Food' (or 'foodstuff'):** Any substance or product, whether processed, partially processed or unprocessed, intended to be ... ingested by humans. 'Food' includes drink, chewing gum and any substance, including water, that is intentionally incorporated into the food during its manufacture, preparation or treatment. It includes bottled drinking water (*Regulation 178/2002* also tells you what is not food!);
- **'Food law':** The laws and regulations governing food in general, and food safety in particular. It covers any stage of production,

processing and distribution of food, and also of feed produced for, or fed to, food-producing animals;

- **'Food business':** Any undertaking, whether for profit or not and whether public or private, carrying out any of the activities related to any stage of production, processing and distribution of food;
- **'Food business operator':** The person(s) responsible for ensuring that the requirements of food law are met within the food business under their control – that's you if you are a food producer!
- **'Food hygiene' or 'hygiene':** The measures and conditions necessary to control hazards and to ensure fitness for human consumption of a foodstuff, taking into account its intended use;
- **'Primary products':** Products of primary production, including products of the soil (growing fruit or vegetables, in other words), of stock farming, of hunting and fishing;
- **'Establishment':** Any unit of a food business;
- **'Competent authority':** The FSAI, HSE, DAFM, FSA, FSS, etc.;
- **'Contamination':** The presence or introduction of a hazard;
- **'Hazard':** Whether physical, chemical or microbiological;
- **'Wrapping':** The placing of a foodstuff in a wrapper or container in direct contact with the foodstuff concerned, and the wrapper or container itself;
- **'Packaging':** The placing of one or more wrapped foodstuffs in a second outer container, and that outer container itself;
- **'Processing':** Any action that substantially alters the initial product, including heating, smoking, curing, maturing, drying, marinating, extraction, extrusion or a combination of those processes;
- **'Unprocessed products':** Foodstuffs that have not undergone processing, and includes products that have been divided, parted, severed, sliced, boned, minced, skinned, ground, cut, cleaned, trimmed, husked, milled, chilled, frozen, deep-frozen or thawed;
- **'Processed products':** Foodstuffs resulting from the processing of unprocessed products. These products may contain ingredients necessary for their manufacture or to give them specific characteristics;
- **'HACCP':** Hazard Analysis and Critical Control Point (see later in this chapter);

- **'Unsafe food':** Article 14 of *Regulation EC 178/2002* requires that food must not be placed on the market if it is unsafe. Food shall be deemed to be unsafe if it is considered to be injurious to health or unfit for human consumption;
- **'Traceability':** Food business operators must be able to identify any person from whom they have been supplied with a food, a food producing animal, or food ingredient. You must have a system and procedures in place to manage your traceability. It's straightforward, but critical (see below for more detail);
- **'The hygiene package':** The bundle of food legislation that applies to ensure consistency and clarity throughout the food production chain, from 'farm to fork'.

## Registration

The law says that, before commencing trading, a food business operator (FBO) – that's you – must register with a competent authority (see above) – that's either with the Environmental Health office in your local HSE (Ireland) or Council (UK and NI) office. Failure to do so is an offence! Businesses that handle and/or process foods of animal origin need approval from the appropriate competent authority, either the DAFM or Council. Once you get in contact, they will go through the details of the approval process with you. In both Ireland and the UK, this can be done online.

If you're not sure which one applies to you, just phone one of them and if it's not them, they'll direct you to the right body. As I've said above, unless you're farm-based or are making cheese for example, it will usually be the EHOs that you need to talk to.

It is really a good idea to contact them for advice sooner rather than later. Approval of your kitchen will take into account the kitchen layout, whether it is easy to clean, where you keep your rubbish (waste management), how you make your foods (processes), food safety (HACCP), your product range and how much you are making (volumes), for a start.

The reason the inspector considers the volume of food you make is that, while you might be able to manage small amounts now, things might get out of control and be hard or impossible to manage if you get too busy. If this busy-ness causes a risk for food safety, then you'll have to make some changes. However, cross that bridge when you come to it. (By the way, being busy because of demand is a good thing for you – it means you are selling lots!).

## Traceability

Traceability is quite simply knowing who you bought your ingredients/foods from and who you sold it on to if you're selling it to another business, such as a restaurant or retailer (B2B). You need this in case of any problem or issue with your foods, so that you can check your records for the specific batch of food in question. Or, as a worst case scenario, in case you have to recall your foods from the market, that you can narrow down the offending batch.

When might this happen? Well, let's say your label omits to mention an allergen in foods you have dispatched, or if you mistakenly include an allergen in a batch of product, then you will have to alert your inspector and they may tell you that you have to recall your foods (nightmare scenario!).

When you're selling directly to the consumer, through a farmers' market or your own shop or in a restaurant (B2C), then you don't need to know the names and addresses of all your customers.

You must keep a list of the suppliers you use regularly (sometimes called an Approved Vendors List). The best way to do this is have a record sheet that you fill every time you buy ingredients or packaging – see www.fsai.ie or www.food.gov.uk for examples or create one yourself.

As a food producer, you should ensure that you use reliable and reputable suppliers and that the products you buy meet your own standards. One way to achieve this is for you to have an agreed product specification with your supplier, including the temperature at which the product must be transported and delivered, the condition of packaging, the correct labelling, and so on.

If you buy poor quality ingredients or raw materials that cause a problem for you in the long run, then it is to you that the customer will complain. It is your reputation that's on the line. The customer is not interested in the fact that one of your suppliers is at fault; all they see is your name on the food that caused illness or problems. So, don't let poor standards from your suppliers result in poor standards for your foods. Also, make sure your suppliers are registered themselves with the HSE or Council, and ask for a copy of their approval certificate for your own files.

In summary:

- All businesses must be able to identify their suppliers (supplier traceability) – what you bought, when you bought it, its batch code and expiry date;
- As a food business supplying your product to other businesses, you must be able to identify your customers (customer traceability);
- Any food placed on the market must be adequately labelled to ensure traceability throughout the food chain – what you sold (an adequate description), when you sold it, its batch code and its expiry date (your shelf life date can sometimes double up as your batch code);
- You must keep the records until you can be reasonably sure the food has been consumed. However, for foods of animal origin, you must keep the records for three years.

*Note:* At the time of writing, *Regulation EC 178/2002* and *Regulation EU 931/2011* apply in the UK too as new legislation post-Brexit has not yet written. However, the same principles are likely to continue to apply, even under new UK legislation. But check! Campden BRI is good for food law alerts (www.campdenbri.co.uk).

## What Is HACCP?

When you are selling food to the general public, you must make sure that your food is safe. In other words, that it won't cause any food poisoning, that it is fit for human consumption and that it is not injurious to health. In order to show that you are in control of what you're doing, then the law (*Regulation EC 852/2004*) says that you must put in some sort of system or procedures to prove it (and if you are dealing with foods of animal origin, then you must also comply with *Regulation EC 853/2004*, don't forget).

HACCP stands for 'Hazard Analysis and Critical Control Point' and is the most common and best-recognised procedure for food safety and hygiene. In the simplest terms, it means that you identify where something might go wrong (that could result in unsafe food) and specify what you would do about it to prevent it from happening. You want to make sure the food is not contaminated by any bacteria or bits of hair or pieces of anything that shouldn't be in there. If it's not in the recipe, it shouldn't be in the food!

If you go to the trouble of putting procedures in place, then for goodness' sake record it and get the credit for it! And if you do record it, make sure it has been done – don't go filling in forms if the job hasn't been done first.

Depending on the food you are producing, the EHO or Inspector may or may not insist that you do formal HACCP training. Look out for courses in your area – see **Chapter 9** for more information.

## HACCP prerequisites

Before implementing HACCP, basic food hygiene conditions and practices referred to as 'prerequisites' must be in place. HACCP then can be used by the business to identify steps that are critical in ensuring the preparation of safe food and which need tight control and monitoring. Prerequisites include:

- **Cleaning and sanitation:** Regular cleaning of premises/equipment;
- **Equipment:** Use equipment that can be thoroughly cleaned and taken apart if necessary;
- **Maintenance:** Repairs and routine maintenance of premises/ equipment;
- **Personal hygiene:** Hand-washing;
- **Pest control:** Vents and any external windows that open in the food preparation areas fitted with a flyscreen/gaps and cracks repaired;
- **Premises and structure:** The size of the premises – your kitchen or garage conversion – must be enough to handle the volume of food you are making;
- **Services:** A potable (safe to drink) water supply – if your water comes from a well or private supply such as a group scheme, then you'll need to get it tested;
- **Storage, distribution and transport:** Storage of foods at the correct temperature/make sure raw and ready-to-eat (RTE) foods are separated;

- **Waste management:** Removing waste frequently to prevent it becoming a source of food contamination – don't let it pile up;
- **Zoning:** Physical separation of activities to prevent potential food contamination – this applies if you are making cooked or other high-risk foods, or if you are washing vegetables.

## Has all this started to put you off yet?

Don't worry, it's really not that difficult to manage all of this when you are operating on a small scale. It looks like a long list but a lot of it is common sense – you are just making sure that there is no dirt that bugs can grow in and that your food won't get contaminated with bacteria or something falling into it. Just make sure everything is clean and tidy, in good order, that you and anyone working with you are also clean and hygienic.

Once you have got the prerequisites sorted, then it is time to get on with looking at the 'seven principles of HACCP'. These are the steps that you take when organising your HACCP plan – get help with this from a training course or food safety advisor or your EHO/Inspector, or from the FSAI or FSA start-up pack. The steps are:

- **Identify the hazards:** If you're lucky, there might not be any;
- **Determine the critical control points (CCPs):** If there is a hazard, what can you do to prevent it becoming a problem for you?
- **Establish critical limit(s):** What's your limit? It might be an upper or lower temperature, for example. Or if you are making high-risk foods that need microbiological testing, then it will be the lab that will let you know what the result is and whether it's a problem;
- **Establish a system to monitor control of the CCPs:** How do you check? Perhaps use a thermometer or a temperature probe for your fridge or for checking the inside of cooked food, for example;
- **Establish the corrective action to be taken when monitoring indicates that a particular CCP is not under control:** If something goes wrong, what do you do? You might just throw it out and start again, you might turn down your fridge temperature setting, or turn up the heat on the cooker, or leave it to cook for longer so that it reaches the right temperature throughout, depending on what it is you are checking up on;

- **Establish procedures for verification to confirm the HACCP system is working effectively:** Do some random spot checks now and then;
- **Establish documentation concerning all procedures and records appropriate to these principles and their application:** Write it all down in your HACCP record forms.

### HACCP records

For HACCP to work successfully and to satisfy the inspectors, records must be kept and be readily available as evidence. The number of records you need will depend very much on the types of foods you are making and complexity of your business. The aim should be to ensure control is maintained without generating excessive paperwork. Ask your EHO or Inspector for guidance.

Again, the *Safe Catering Pack* is very handy for learning about HACCP and gives you all the forms you need to keep your records. FSAI also has a booklet, *HACCP Terminology Explained*, that you can download free from its website – and you can download all the record forms free there too. FSA has a very good free guide, *Food Hygiene: A Guide for Businesses*, on its website and a great online tool, MyHACCP. Don't panic, it's not rocket science!

## Low Risk & High Risk

A low-risk food is one that is unlikely to be a risk to public health – in other words, cause food poisoning – usually because they are acidic (like pickle) or don't contain much water (like bread or jam) so bacteria can't grow easily. Low-risk foods spoil due to their chemical composition (not microbiological activity) and usually have a 'Best Before' date. Bread, cake, buns, jam are all low-risk generally.

High-risk foods, on the other hand, are much more at risk of microbial contamination, particularly harmful bacteria called pathogens. These foods are generally refrigerated or frozen, and have a 'Use By' date. Examples include seafood, freshly prepared salads, or ready-to-eat foods such as quiche, cooked foods, some meats and dairy products. The main reason these are high-risk is because they may be eaten without any further cooking or processing, so if they are contaminated with food poisoning bacteria, then the consumer is at risk. However, even if the food is going to be cooked by the consumer before it is eaten, it is also considered high-risk.

If you have a sponge cake that you sandwich together with a fresh cream filling, it increases the risk. The sponge itself is low-risk, but because the cream is a dairy product and can go off (spoilage bacteria will grow) unless it's refrigerated, then that increases the risk. When to use Best Before and Use By dates is covered in **Chapter 7**.

## TACCP & VACCP

Just when you thought there couldn't be anything more to think about then you hear these two terms – TACCP and VACCP:

- Threat Assessment and Critical Control Points (TACCP) focuses on tampering, intentional adulteration of food, and food defence.
- Vulnerability Assessment and Critical Control Points (VACCP) also focuses on food fraud but widens the scope to include the prevention of any potential adulteration of food, whether or not intentional, by identifying the vulnerable points in a supply chain.

These are not legal requirements, but might be something to consider in the future as your business grows.

## Conclusion

It's understandable that a new producer just starting up may find the legislation all a bit overwhelming. Don't feel you need to know the legislation inside out and have it all at your fingertips. Just know what you need for your foods.

But that's the problem! How do I know what I need for my food? Ask your EHO or Inspector for advice. You can also ask your Local Enterprise Office (www.localenterprise.ie) or Enterprise Unit in your Council to give you a food business mentor (this is often a free service) – just make sure your mentor knows the legislation. You'll get to know it all yourself well enough in good time.

# 4

# ENSURING FOOD SAFETY & HYGIENE

## Basic Microbiology

A micro-organism (microbe) is a creature that is invisible to the human eye and can be seen only under a microscope. A dot on a page the size of a full stop would contain millions of them. Microbes are found everywhere – in your hair, throat, nose, gut and hands; in the soil and air; on surfaces; in food, shellfish, water, vegetables, plants … and the word used to describe this is 'ubiquitous'.

There are five types: bacteria, viruses, moulds, yeasts and fungi. Some of these microbes are useful and good for us – for example:

- Bacteria (*Lactobacilli*) aid digestion;
- Fungi (mushrooms) are edible;
- Moulds produce antibiotics (penicillin), and are used in making cheese (Brie rind);
- Viruses are used to make vaccines and in immunotherapy;
- Yeasts are used in brewing beer, baking bread and other fermented foods.

Most bacteria are harmless but many are responsible for disease, illness and infection. Harmful bacteria are known as pathogens:

- Bacteria (sometimes called 'germs' or 'bugs') can cause food poisoning and thus illness;
- Fungi cause food spoilage;

- Moulds also cause food spoilage (for example, on bread or cheese);
- Viruses can cause food poisoning;
- Yeasts – too many can contaminate liquids.

Many bacteria are capable of forming spores – a protective shell that helps them to survive when food is scarce. You are probably familiar with tetanus or 'lock jaw'. Tetanus is an infection of the nervous system by the potentially deadly bacteria *Clostridium tetani*. Spores of the bacteria live in the soil. In the spore form, *C. tetani* may remain inactive in the soil, as if it is hibernating, but it can remain infectious for more than 40 years. So that's why if you get soil in a cut, you need to wash it out straight away, or get a tetanus shot, just in case.

## What do bacteria need to grow?

Bacteria need six things to grow:

- **Time:** Bacteria divide in half (and so double in number) every 20 minutes under the right conditions;
- **Warmth:** The best temperature for them to grow is 37°C (body temperature) but they can grow in temperatures anywhere from 5°C to 63°C, known as the 'danger zone';
- **Oxygen:** For some bacteria (aerobic), but others grow without it (anaerobic bacteria);
- **Food:** Protein, which could be proper food or just dirt;
- **Moisture:** Water;
- **pH (acid/alkali conditions):** Bacteria dislike extremes so they won't grow where it's too acidic (on pickles) or too alkaline (which is why soap works to clean them away).

## How do I control the growth of bacteria?

Simply put, if you can control some or all of the six things above – time, warmth, oxygen, food, moisture and pH – then you will do well.

As a rule of thumb, keep hot food hot, keep cold food cold (refrigerated at 5°C or below). Food must be cooked to 75°C or hotter. Do not leave hot food sitting around for too long where it will start to cool; if the temperature of the food is at less than 63°C for more than two hours, then you have to throw it out. Put food in the fridge as soon as possible.

You might preserve some foods by removing oxygen (for example, by bottling it, or putting it in jars, or canning it). Lack of moisture in some foods will prevent bacteria growing in them (jam, preserves, dried foods). Vegetables can be preserved by controlling the pH, which is how pickling developed (the acid in the vinegar isn't suitable for most bacteria to grow). Finally, preserving foods by smoking (for example, smoked salmon) is one of the world's oldest methods of slowing microbial growth. However, smoking alone isn't usually sufficient to get any decent shelf life and is usually helped by vacuum packing.

Don't feed the bugs (clean to remove dirt) and don't leave damp cleaning cloths or mops about where bugs can start to grow.

### What are some common types of bacteria?

You might have heard of *Salmonella, E. coli, Clostridium perfringens* (one of the main causes of food poisoning), *Clostridium difficile* (sometimes referred to as *C. diff.*) which is a hospital-acquired infection, *Clostridium botulinum* (causes botulism – also used in Botox, by the way, as it acts by paralysing the muscle), *Campylobacter, Staphylococcus* or *Streptococcus*.

Most *E. coli* strains are harmless, but some can cause serious food poisoning. The harmless strains are part of the normal flora of the gut. The bad news is that, even if the harmless ones are found in food, it shows that the food has been contaminated with faeces. Yuck!

Most *Staphylococci* are harmless and are normally found on the skin and mucous membranes of humans (inside the nose) and other animals. So, if it's in your food, it possibly means that someone hasn't been washing their hands after blowing their nose. Eeeooow!

While many types of *Streptococcus* are harmless, you will be familiar with the one that causes 'Strep throat'. If *Streptococcus* is found in your food, it possibly means that someone may have coughed into your food or hasn't been washing their hands after coughing. Not nice!

### What is food poisoning?

Food poisoning is an illness that occurs usually between six and 36 hours after eating poisonous or contaminated food. Symptoms include vomiting, nausea, diarrhoea, abdominal pain and even death in extreme cases.

Food poisoning can be caused by bacteria, viruses, chemicals, metals (such as lead or mercury) and poisonous plants, such as the foxglove (digitalis) or poisonous mushrooms or toadstools.

## How do I reduce bacteria in the food I make?

There are three ways to reduce bacteria in the food you make:

- **Food hygiene management:** To make sure the food does not get contaminated;
- **Personal hygiene management:** Keeping yourself and your staff /helpers clean;
- **Environmental hygiene management:** Keeping your equipment, and workplace clean and tidy.

Each of these will be controlled by your HACCP system that we discussed earlier. When you do your food hygiene training (which is required by law), then all will be explained in more detail.

# Case Study: John & Maria's Wedding

I attended the wedding of friends a few years ago in England. The reception was held in their local village hall and the food – a buffet of cold meats and salads – was catered by family and friends.

The next day, all 58 guests, and the newly married couple, suffered a really bad dose of food poisoning. Four people were hospitalised, as they were severely ill. Due to the large number of people affected, the incident was notified to Staffordshire Council and an investigation ensued.

The offending food was not identified, which meant no finger pointing at the unfortunate person who had prepared it, but it was most likely a pasta salad, where the pasta was not completely cold before being mixed with mayonnaise or tuna or meat.

It just shows that food poisoning can happen easily and can just as easily affect a large number of people. Bad enough that this would happen at a wedding, but just imagine if this was your food business!

# Hygiene

Hygiene refers to the practices and procedures essential to the maintenance of health and the quality of life – keeping things clean and uncontaminated, in other words.

## Why bother?

If you don't have good hygiene practices when you prepare food, then you run the risk of causing food poisoning. That's not good for your customer and not good for your reputation or your business.

## Personal hygiene

Good personal hygiene includes keeping your body clean (shower regularly), washing your hands regularly, wearing clean clothes and not engaging in unhygienic practices such as smoking, coughing or sneezing over food or people, picking your nose, ears, cuts, etc., nail-biting, using your finger to taste food, double-dipping (using a spoon to taste, licking it, then dipping the same spoon into the food again without washing it first) or spitting.

The big thing to remember here is WASH YOUR HANDS!

You must always wash your hands:

- **Before:**
  - o Starting work;
  - o Handling food;
  - o You move on to the next task;
- **Before and after:**
  - o Treating wounds or cuts;
  - o Touching a sick or injured person;
  - o Inserting or removing contact lenses;
- **After:**
  - o Using the toilet;
  - o Handling raw food, especially meat;
  - o Touching your face, nose, ears, hair, mouth, cuts;
  - o Smoking;
  - o Handling waste;
  - o Cleaning duties;

o   Meal breaks;

o   Sneezing, coughing, or blowing your nose;

o   Handling money (just think about where money has been!)

A carrier is a person who harbours, and may pass on, harmful bacteria, even though that person may show no signs of illness. If this person has poor personal hygiene and they handle food, then they might easily pass on the harmful bacteria to someone else.

## Accreditation

There are several accreditation schemes that you may like to sign up for once your business is established.

In Ireland, look at the Bord Bia Quality Assurance Scheme, which is for beef, lamb and poultry farmers, egg producers, retail butchers, dairy, horticulture and others (www.bordbia.ie/farmersgrowers/get-involved/become-quality-assured/).

Organic accreditation is covered in **Chapter 6**.

Several schemes in the UK are listed in **Chapter 16**, such as SALSA, Red Tractor and British Retail Consortium (BRC). Irish producers who wish to sell to the larger UK retailers will need to have BRC at some point.

# 5

# PRODUCT DEVELOPMENT

## Introduction

Wherever you get your ideas or whatever your motivation, you need to think things through before ploughing ahead. The more time, thought and energy that you give to this at the start, then the higher your chances of success.

Your resources (financial, human, facilities) are limited, especially at the beginning of a project. So, it is important to spend resources wisely: by being careful from the start, you will ensure that there will be enough time, cash and energy to keep going.

Questions you should consider:

- **What are you going to make/produce/sell?** This is your first priority. Be clear what you want to do and why you want to do it. It will work out best if you enjoy what you are doing, and are good at it. Ideally, when looking at the local market, see if there is a gap that you can fill with your delicious food. For example, despite competition, there are still market opportunities for Irish ice cream-makers. Ice cream is often regarded as an 'affordable indulgence' and suits the trend towards home entertainment;

- **Who/what is your target market?** Is it families, individuals, older people, children, single people, married couples, men, women, healthy eaters, dieters, indulgers, students, workers ...? Don't make the mistake of thinking that everyone is your target market. Different groups like different things;

- **Who are your competitors?** Everyone has a competitor. Even makers of sausages with high meat content have competition from poorer quality sausages – if the consumer is offered a choice, they may go for the cheaper option, despite it being lower quality, depending on their budget. Know who your competitors are, where they are, and how you might steal away some of their customers! Carry out a benchmarking exercise: What do your competitors do well that you might do too, and what are their weaknesses? You can compete with them by shouting about your strengths, the great traits/flavours/quality of your food;

- **How will you make the cheese/bread/jam/hummus?** Can you get the necessary ingredients? Do you want to use organic ingredients? Will your customers pay extra for them? Will changing an ingredient impact positively or negatively on your food – will it taste better or worse? Have you a recipe and method? Does it work for bigger batches?

- **What equipment/premises are needed?** Do you need any specialised equipment? Will your existing kitchen equipment do or must you buy new equipment? Do you need a new fridge? Have you enough cupboard space? Is everything cleanable? (See **Chapter 3**);

- **Where will your food be sold?** You could start by providing a local service to build recognition – collections from your house, deliver to local shops or supermarkets, sell at farmers'/country markets and agricultural shows and music/cultural events. Sell online. Where do your competitors sell their goods? Will you be there too? (See **Chapter 6**);

- **How much should you charge?** You need to compare the selling price of your food to similar products on the market. The consumer may expect to pay more for artisan food, but you need to prove it's worth the extra. Also, make sure you are not undercharging – don't forget to work out how much it costs you to make it (ingredients, electricity, packaging, your time, distribution) so that you don't make a loss (see **Chapter 8**);

- **Where and when will the food be eaten?** Meal times, picnics, on-the-go, special occasions … this will affect the way you present and package the food, whether you put one, two or six items in a pack for example, as well as the type of packaging itself. If the travelling public is your market, eating on-the-go or 'dashboard dining', then remember to think about what portion size and packaging will best suit someone having lunch at their desk or in their car;

- **What are your packaging options?** Can you use plastic, paper, recyclable/green credentials, glass, jars, tubs or bags? How many items should you put in a pack? Should you offer the option of single packs and multi-packs? If your food is already in shops, think about pack sizes, formats and packaging for existing lines;

- **Is the product seasonal?** How do you manage in winter or offseason? Can you buy-in ingredients from elsewhere when you don't have them in your own garden, for example? Can you adapt the product for different times of year? Can you introduce limited edition or seasonal varieties such as a turkey and ham pie at Christmas, lamb and mint for Easter, or bacon and cabbage for St. Patrick's Day?

- **How much of an income can you hope to get from making and selling these foods?** Is this going to be extra money for you or do you want to have a business that will provide you with a proper income? Either way, you must work out your costs (this is all covered in detail in **Chapter 8**).

## New Product Development

Once you decide what it is you want to make, it is really important that you spend enough time developing your recipe and method. Do plenty of trials to make sure you can manage making bigger batches, more than one or two at a time. Your kitchen equipment might be fine at the beginning, but might not last if you are using it long-term or for larger sizes/quantities. Or your recipe may not scale – for example, if you increase the size of a cake from 6″ to 9″ or 12″, and you use the same recipe, it might not turn out the same. You may have to alter your recipe and method for larger sizes – trial and error again.

You might have heard about new product development (NPD) models or perhaps the phrase 'stage gate'. These are just ways of managing the way in which new foods, or indeed any new products, are developed. The idea is to make sure you avoid wasting your resources (time, energy, money, mental health!) as far as you can.

Typical stages are:

- **Idea generation:** How to come up with new ideas (see above);
- **Feasibility:** Desk research, check out the market – is there anyone else local doing what you want to do? Look at your resources: do you have the time, money, knowledge, ability, kitchen, equipment etc. that you need? Perhaps you should do a full-scale feasibility study before going too much further. Consider the following:
  - *Technical* – can I make it?
    - Product development;
    - Operations;
  - *Commercial* – can I sell it?
    - Target market;
    - Routes to market;
    - Distribution;
  - *Financial* – can I make a profit?
    - Costs;
    - Sales projections;
    - Cash flows;
    - Profit & loss;
  - *Team* – who is going to do it?
    - Third parties;
    - Roles and responsibilities;
    - Risk analysis.
- **Concept development:** Produce samples, do trials, test them out on your family and friends. Move on to bigger batches, check any technical issues (again, you may need to tweak your recipe);
- **Business case:** This stage includes a more detailed look at your target market, sales (how and where are you going to sell your food?), production (how and where are you going to make it?), human

resources (will it be just you or will you have help, and who is going to do what?) and financial issues (can you afford to start-up? Can you get a grant? What are your financial projections and what about cash flow?) (see **Chapter 8** for more about money);

- **Launch:** Introduce your new product to the market – in effect, this probably means putting a few loaves, jars, buns, cakes or whatever into your car or the basket of your bicycle and bringing them to the corner shop where your local friendly shopkeeper has agreed to take a few to try them out and see whether they sell;

- **Review:** Look back over everything now and then and see whether you want to make any changes. Can you get cheaper/better ingredients? Can you make bigger batches? Can you add to the range? Can you save on costs anywhere without compromising your quality?

## Outsourcing Production

Processing partners/third party manufacturing/co-packing – these are all terms that are used to describe outsourcing production. It is not unreasonable to consider outsourcing some or all of your production work. For example, you could buy readymade pastry instead of making your own. It is possible to buy very good quality frozen pastry, so don't rule it out. Some of the top chefs in the country buy-in their pastry!

If you are making sausages or meat products, you might develop the recipe and specify the ingredients, but perhaps you don't have a sausage machine. You could ask a butcher to make the sausages for you or ask if you can have access to the machine when it's not in use.

Another option is to send your foods to a packaging or bottling specialist (co-packing/co-packaging). Canning and bottling lines are expensive pieces of equipment and these are not investments that small breweries or drinks producers could afford or justify. There are contract bottlers and canning operators located across the country. Alternatively, some drinks producers who have available capacity on their canning/bottling line may be happy to earn money providing their facilities to others when they're not using it themselves. Just phone them up and ask!

You might even outsource your order fulfilment if you are selling online. What this means is that you don't have your own warehouse where you have to run around and select products to post off to the consumer who has bought them online. Instead, someone else picks, packs, and ships your online orders to customers. The foods are kept in a warehouse elsewhere, and orders are shipped from there (we are talking big volumes here, of course).

To take it a step further, you could outsource everything, the entire production process. Supermarket own brands do this all the time. If your business grows to a point where you want to focus on sales and marketing, then that may be the time to get a third party producer do the making for you. There are some producers who only make for others and sell nothing under their own name at all

The golden rule of any 'partnership' is trust and making sure that you can work with people for the long-term. The trust derived from business relationships offers far more security than anything written down in a contract. All the same, you should ask your sub-contractor (the person/company who is going to make the food for you) to sign a non-disclosure agreement, which would give you some protection, but you should be aware that even a slight tweak to a recipe or a process might render this agreement null and void.

One step you should definitely take is to document your recipe and the detail of the required processes and send both to yourself by registered post and DO NOT OPEN the envelope unless you find yourself in a litigation process and only then open the package in a legal setting – solicitor's office or courtroom – with independent witnesses present. This is a simple and cost-effective method of proving ownership of the intellectual property (IP) for small businesses. Get legal advice about this though, to make sure you cover yourself.

## Sensory Analysis

How does the food taste, look, smell and feel? Dark chocolate snaps when you break it because it has a high percentage of cocoa solids. Or does anyone remember Space Rocks, which popped and fizzed in your mouth? The smell of bread evokes feelings and memories of well-being for people. When we smell bread, the olfactory bulb, which starts inside the nose and runs along the bottom of the brain, has direct connections to the two brain areas that are strongly connected to emotion and memory. These are called the 'organoleptic' properties of food and assessing them is what we call 'sensory analysis'.

If you ever watch cookery programmes on television, you might notice that the good chefs taste their food as they go along. They want to make sure that there is a good balance of flavours, that it is seasoned correctly, that no one ingredient is overpowering – and they make adjustments accordingly. The same goes for the foods you are making for your new business.

Sensory analysis of food uses the five senses – sight, smell, taste, touch and hearing – either individually or in combination, to look at the characteristics of food:

- Appearance (sight);
- Flavour (taste and touch);
- Aroma (smell);
- Texture or 'mouthfeel' (touch)
- Sound (hearing).

## Appearance

We eat with our eyes first, so is your food visually appealing? Think about the colour, size, shape and shine. The colour of food is very important: does it look natural or artificial? Bright green vegetables look fresher, for example. The shape, size and appearance also influence consumers. When is mould acceptable? Fine in a blue cheese but not on bread! Wilted lettuce or carrots that have a wizened appearance are not acceptable either. Good chocolate should be shiny, not dull.

## Flavour

The flavour of food is detected by the taste buds on the tongue and is actually a combination of taste and touch / texture. There are four types of taste sensation: sweet; salt; sour; and bitter.

Sour and bitter tastes are often confused, so you need to be clear what your tasters mean when they describe the taste to you. Lemon juice has a sour taste, whereas coffee has a bitter taste.

## Aroma

Smell detects the aroma of food – the smell of freshly-baked cakes, coffee brewing, lemon, garlic or bacon frying, for example – and is important in the appreciation of flavour.

A pleasant aroma makes food appetising.

Smell is also useful in detecting fresh, rancid or occasionally poisonous food.

## Texture/mouthfeel

Texture – how the food feels in your mouth – is a key quality for many foods. For example, think of the tenderness of meat, the crunch when breaking into a *crème brulée* or the chewiness of toffee. It includes the consistency, viscosity (thick or thin liquids), brittleness, chewiness and the size and shape of particles in food, like lumpy mashed potato or the texture of a pear that is gritty. The coldness of ice cream or the burning sensation of chilli are also considered to be textures, and they contribute to the overall flavour.

## Sound

The sounds made by food during preparation and while eating it are important for consumers' decisions also – like the sizzle of fried food, the fizz of drinks, the crunch of raw vegetables, the cracking of hard biscuits or dark chocolate.

## Sensory analysis testing

It is really very important to taste your food, to get others to taste it and give you feedback, and then to adjust your recipe as necessary. Ideally, your tasters would be able to describe what they are tasting rather than simply saying they like it or don't like it without articulating why. You might do this when developing new products, for example, or if you've changed an ingredient and want to assess the impact of that, if you're trying to eliminate an ingredient for some reason and are using a flavouring instead, or if you want to measure or benchmark your foods against a competitor.

To do this properly, you should set up a 'Sensory Analysis/Taste' panel. This can be formal or informal, depending on your resources.

You might decide to do it yourself (in-house) or maybe it would be better to get someone else to facilitate it to ensure objectivity.

Broadly speaking, sensory analysis can be divided into:

- **Difference/discrimination tests:**
  - Can they detect a difference between the foods?
  - How noticeable is the difference, if any?
  - If so, describe the difference? For example, stronger, weaker, sweeter, more sour...
- **Preference tests, also called affective or consumer tests:**
  - Do they like the product?
  - Which one do they prefer?
  - Would they buy it?
- **Descriptive analysis (trained panels):**
  - What does it taste like?
  - Describe the taste;
  - What are the characteristics of its Appearance, Flavour, Smell, Texture or Sound (if relevant)?

A word of warning! Sometimes family / friends do not make good taste testers as they don't want to say they dislike something for fear of offending you! Whoever you choose, make sure they'll be honest, that they can articulate what they sense, and also that you're open to criticism! Put some questions together to ensure you get the information you need. You can use a trained panel, and these can be accessed through specialist services in universities, catering colleges or through private services (see **Chapter 17**).

Smokers do not make good tasters, by the way, as their taste buds are not sensitive enough. Ensure any coffee drinkers brush their teeth and rinse their mouths out well with water before starting.

## Shelf Life

When you have developed your recipe, and are happy with the end result, you will have to work out the Best Before or Use By date for the label. One of the best explanations I've heard to describe the difference between 'Best Before' and 'Use By' dates is that used by *safe*food: Best Before is a guideline and Use By is a deadline (www.safefood.eu)

Shelf life tells the consumer how long food can be kept before it starts to deteriorate. However, it is up to the consumer to follow the stated storage conditions if the shelf life is to be achieved.

## Is shelf life related to food quality?

Yes, the food might be safe to eat after the expiry (Best Before) date, but it might be stale or mushy or flavourless. Since the Best Before date is related to quality (for example, taste, aroma, appearance), after that date the food may not be unsafe to eat, but it may not be pleasant to eat either.

Best Before is applied to foods that are low risk or are canned, frozen or dried, for example – usually foods that have a long shelf life. Foods that have passed the Best Before date can be sold, provided the consumer is made aware.

## Is shelf life related to food safety?

Yes, absolutely! You use HACCP (**Chapter 3**) to help control the growth of pathogens (bad bacteria). The Use By date is all about the safety of a food product. In other words, is it safe to eat? It is very important for perishable foods that may pose a danger to human health after a short time. The accuracy of the Use By date is really important from a food safety point of view.

Foods with a Use By date generally have a short shelf life. Foods that have passed the Use By date cannot be sold.

## How to work out the shelf life of your food

Shelf life testing works out how long a food will retain its quality during storage. The extent to which you have to do a 'shelf life study' depends on the food you are producing. Factors influencing shelf life of food include microbial growth (mould, bacteria, yeasts, etc.) and nonmicrobial spoilage caused due to the gain or loss of moisture from the food; any chemical changes that might occur; light-induced change (colour fading); temperature changes (which cause the whitening or 'bloom' in chocolate); physical damage that might occur over time if it gets crumbly or cracks form; or even other spoilage from rodents and insects, taint or tampering.

All these factors should be taken into account when working out your shelf life. If you are making low-risk foods like bread, jam, or dips, where public health is not a major issue, your own experience will inform you as to what the shelf life might be. For high-risk foods, though, you will have to send samples away to a microbiology lab for testing to measure how many bacteria are present that you need to worry about. Check with your inspector if you're unsure as to whether you need to test your foods.

Can you carry out your own shelf life testing? Yes, you can do it easily for some types of foods, especially those where it's the eating quality that you are concerned about. Simply store the food in its packaging under the storage conditions it should be kept in, then take a sample every day or week or as often as you need to notice any changes. This will give you a guide as to when the food starts to deteriorate, and you can set the shelf life accordingly. If you're not sure, or if your food is perishable and where food safety is the issue, then get professional advice.

By law, you must state the Best Before or Use By date on your label. This is covered in detail in **Chapter 7**.

# 6

# ROUTES TO MARKET, BRANDING & MARKETING

---

## What is a Route to Market?

The 'route to market' is how you get your food onto consumers' tables, whether directly or through shops.

The first step in finding the best routes to market for you is to think about the food itself, and what might suit it. Think about who you want to sell it to: they are your target customer. Is this for consumers? For the hospitality or food service sector? For retail? For web sales? Or a combination of these?

You should write down a short statement or business pitch that you will use to all your potential business customers and retailers. It's good to prepare this in advance and be very familiar with it yourself, since it will help you to be consistent rather than stumbling over your words every time you try to talk to someone about your new food venture. Include a clear description of the food's unique selling points (USPs). Practice saying it out loud, to hear how it sounds.

The location and nature of your target market will influence which route to market you use. For most small-scale producers, the market is usually their local or regional area to begin with, selling to consumers who prefer local food and who are willing to pay a premium for it.

# Where Are Your Customers?

Before you even start thinking about your best route to market, ask:

- Where do my potential customers shop? If you only sell in Farmers' and Country markets, are you missing out on a large number of shoppers who only shop in supermarkets?
- Where are people going anyway that you might be able to sell from?
- Is your food suitable for people on the go? If so, service stations with convenience shops are the places to market your products.

Consider regional airports, where travellers are always keen to take something back home either for themselves or to bring as a gift; tourist attractions where there are large numbers of people herding through the gift shops and cafés; museums ... could you sell there? Well, you won't know unless you ask!

# The Supply Chain

It is important for food businesses to understand the supply chain with which they are involved. There are usually two types:

- Retailers (for consumer foods) – B2B2C;
- Food service (business to business or catering) – B2B.

Alternative supply chains involve direct sales to consumers and many small producers start with this route – because it is short and simple. Direct sales can include farmers' markets and online selling.

The diagram on the next page shows two typical supply chains and the three steps in the process between farm and consumer: each step in the process takes a slice of the 'money pie'. By using the direct sales route, some of the steps are eliminated, and with them, some of the costs.

# Route Options – Direct & Indirect

There are two main routes to market categories:

- **Direct sales – from you direct to the consumer (direct customer – B2C):**
  o  Country/Farmers' markets;
  o  Online (e-commerce)/telephone sales;

- o  Farm shop/self-collection by consumers;
- o  Agricultural/County Shows;
- o  Weddings and celebrations/events/concerts;
- **Indirect sales – from you to your business customer (B2B or B2B2C):**
  - o  Supermarkets;
  - o  Distributors, agents and wholesalers;
  - o  Food service (hotels, cafés, restaurants, pubs, catering, service station forecourts);
  - o  Independent retailers/specialist shops/artisan outlets.

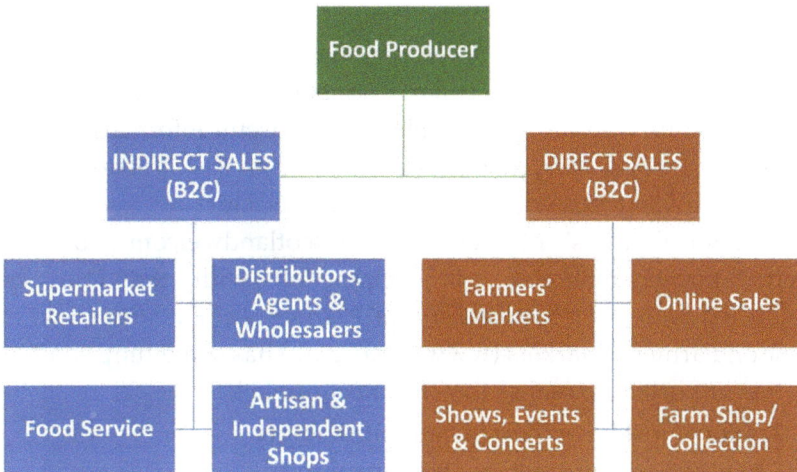

## Direct Sales

### *Farmers' & Country markets*

Farmers' (outdoor) and Country (indoor) markets provide direct access to customers. This route is good for getting customer feedback and for carrying out initial tests of market/product and a great many small producers use this route to market successfully. Farmers' markets attract local trade, bringing consumers who are concerned about mass-produced food, about supporting local producers, and who are keen to minimise food miles. These consumers are willing to pay extra for these benefits. These are the 'foodies'.

According to Bord Bia, at the last count, there were approximately 175 Farmers' and Country markets operating in Ireland (up from 130 four years ago), nine more in Northern Ireland (www.discovernorthernireland.com), over 30 in Wales (www.welshcountry.co.uk/farmersmarkets-in-wales/) and at least 52 in Scotland (www.scotlandwelcomesyou.com/scottish-farmers-markets/). In London alone, there are 19 (London Farmers' Markets/www.lfm.org.uk).

The successful markets get plenty of customers (good footfall), attract regular customers who buy every week, have producers that offer good quality foods for sale consistently and are well-managed.

If you decide to try this route, then you need to be aware of the rules and regulations that markets apply to producers. In Ireland, there is a *Voluntary Code of Good Practice for Farmers' Markets* available from Bord Bia (www.bordbia.ie). Bord Bia also publishes *A Guide to Selling through Farmers' Markets, Farm Shops & Box Schemes in Ireland*, which again you can find on its website. There is also lots of useful information in *The Village Market Handbook*, downloadable free from Irish Village Markets (www.irishvillagemarkets.ie) or FSAI (www.fsai.ie).

Scottish Farmers' Markets (www.scotlandwelcomesyou.com/scottish-farmers-markets/), in conjunction with the FSA, has published *Selling at a Scottish Farmers' Market – The First Steps*, and the London Farmers' Markets (www.lfm.org.uk) has something similar.

It is important to realise that, for most markets:

- Traders must have their own public liability insurance – see **Chapter 8** for information about insurance;
- Not all markets provide canopies and tables, so you might have to bring your own every time;
- Traders involved in the handling of food must comply with food safety legislation, of course, and some markets may ask you to show your HACCP approval certificate. There are some published guidelines for food stalls, so ask your Council Inspector or EHO.

Standing at a food stall is labour-intensive – and it's hard on the feet! It requires commitment in terms of stall staffing and management – and cash handing may be a risk factor.

From the perspective of the small food producer, direct selling via farmers' markets, box schemes and farm shops offers a number of advantages as a route to market. The supply chain is relatively short and there is direct contact with customers. This is a good way to start to build relationships with your customers, who will then recognise your food when they see it in their local shops. It also allows you to display your food the way you want it displayed, as you're not relying on shops to do the job for you.

For the direct sales route, investment in equipment may be required and might include, as well as the table/canopy, a mobile refrigerated unit and utensils if you need them, plates for samples, a tablecloth and so on. Transport requirements are generally far simpler than the more conventional routes to market and there are usually no intermediaries involved. In other words, you bring it all in your own car/van/trailer/bicycle!

Recently I have noticed that some market traders are offering the facility to take card payments, not just cash, and I would heartily recommend that you consider doing this too – it removes another barrier to selling as many people just don't carry cash any more. And it's more secure – revenue from card payments is less easily stolen than cash.

## E-commerce/online

E-commerce/online sales have grown massively as a direct route to consumers, especially in the last three years. During the lock-downs of Covid-19, when hotels and restaurants were closed, some food producers lost up to 70% of their trade and needed to find alternative customers to fill the considerable gaps that were left. Since consumers were not going out or away on holiday back then, they were cooking much more at home and had time to spend on trying out new foods and recipes. (When was there ever so much sourdough bread made?!)

In March 2020, I compiled a list of food producers in Ireland who had e-commerce enabled on-line shops at that time and could only find about 40. Now, there are over 275 that I am aware of – and counting. Producers have invested time and money into getting their e-commerce house in order. While such reliance on-line sales has diminished, it is still an important route to market for many producers.

When it comes to delivering your foods that have been ordered online, there are a few considerations, and packaging is critical. Can you protect your foods enough against damage during transport? Can you maintain the right temperatures for chilled foods (the chill-chain)? Can you use sustainable packaging? Can you sell a mixed variety of flavours? Online sales are bound to continue to grow as consumers love the convenience, so make sure you offer a reliable and prompt service.

I first came across online ordering for meal delivery services capitalising on the growth of the health, convenience and fitness trends in London a few years ago and it has really taken off in in Ireland too. Examples include Drop Chef (Ireland) (www.dropchef.com) or Hello Fresh (Ireland and UK) (www.hellofresh.ie, www.hellofresh.co.uk), both of which deliver full meal kits. In the UK, there's also Cookaway (www.thecookaway.com), Mindful Chef (www.mindfulchef.com) and many others, as convenience is always sought after by busy people who still like to cook for themselves.

There are costs associated with online sales, with website design and maintenance to be considered. Nonetheless, some producers *only* sell online, while other producers provide an ordering service by telephone.

It has often been suggested that the delivery of orders from online or telephone sales could be managed on a rotation basis by a group of motivated producers in a local area. However, despite many examples of where such a delivery network has been set up, most don't survive unless one person takes control of the managing orders and organising the deliveries. Frankly, this rarely works out. The person needs to be paid, then there's the management of all that, and in the end most producers just arrange or deliver all their own produce themselves.

Alternatively, the consumer might collect their order either from the producer, farm-gate/house/shop, or from a central distribution point like NeighbourFood in Ireland, Scotland and England (www.neighbourfood.ie and www.neighbourfood.co.uk).

More recently, online shops have been set up which producers can use to help get their foods to market. Examples of these are the award-winning IndieFude (www.indiefude.com) in Northern Ireland or My Caboose Store (www.mycaboosestore.ie) and Craft Food Traders (www.craftfoodtraders.ie). Amazon is a good outlet too for food (www.sell.amazon.de/en or www.sell.amazon.co.uk). At the time of writing, Amazon announced that a dedicated website for Ireland (www.amazon.ie) will start in 2025.

There are some on-line platforms that help suppliers to connect with retail buyers, and vice versa. Two examples are Kwayga (www.kwayga.com) and Range Me (www.rangeme.com).

Many speciality retailers have their own online shops, as do the multiple retailers, so talk to the relevant buyers about opportunities.

Hampers can be a source of volume for sales, especially at Christmas. However, it can be difficult to win a listing, and the margins are not as good as retail. That said, for the volume you'll sell, the margin cut might be worth it. Examples of hamper companies include Gifts Direct (www.giftsdirect.com), Hampers & Co. (www.hampersandco.com) or Irish Gourmet (www.irishgourmet.ie).

Speciality shops also sell hampers, so contact them. Examples include Café Rua's 'Bosca Rua' (www.caferua.com), Shell's Café (www.shellscafe.com), Ardkeen Stores (www.ardkeen.com) or McCambridge's (www.mccambridges.com), but there are many, many more across Ireland, Northern Ireland and the UK.

## Agricultural shows & festivals

Agricultural shows and seasonal festivals are a great way to get your food produce to your customers. There are many annual markets and fairs, summer and Christmas food festivals. Huge crowds attend rural Agricultural and County Shows in Ireland and the UK, so be sure to check them out as they usually have a dedicated food producers section (www.irishshows.org and www.asao.co.uk/events).

In Ireland, the National Ploughing Championships attracts crowds of up to 280,000 people across three days in September every year! (www.npa.ie). People attend these shows with the intention of spending money, they're a captive audience, and while it might be expensive to book a stall, it generally is worth your while. Events like these provide a chance for consumers to try out new products, and for producers to test the market without having to make a longer-term commitment to a market, week in week out.

## Other

Other direct routes to market include:

- **Weddings:** If you plan to make products for the wedding market, then it's wedding fairs you should target, as well as shops selling wedding dresses, suit hire, florists or anything associated with the event – and don't forget hen parties, where chocolate and confectionary work particularly well;

- **Celebrations:** If you plan to make celebration cakes for birthdays, anniversaries, religious occasions, retirements etc., then leave cards or flyers in children's play centres, children's clothes shops, baby equipment retailers, gift shops and so on;
- **Concerts:** Outdoor concert events continue to grow and, if you are in the food service business and can feed a crowd, then these might offer you a good way to get your foods to the masses, and market yourself at the same time;
- **Corporate events:** Businesses often run events for their employees and look for something different to offer. If you have a food truck or are in the Street Food business, then marketing to this sector is a good way to get business.

The direct route to market is also labour-intensive and requires good organisation and management, and a strong commitment from producers who are willing to travel and manage orders and deliveries.

Regardless of whatever direct routes you choose, and you might try out a few over the years, then social media marketing is essential to ensure consumers are aware of you beforehand. We will talk more about social and digital media later in this chapter.

## Indirect Sales

Route to market options for indirect sales:
- Supermarket chains – the 'multiples';
- Distributors, agents and wholesalers;
- Food service;
- Specialist shops / independent retailers / artisan outlets.

### Supermarket chains

Selling through supermarket chains might sound like a dream come true. Yes, the footfall of customers is much greater than you could ever hope for through direct sales as I've described above, but there are several considerations you should be aware of before going down this road. In fact, the phrase "be careful what you wish for" is apt here:

- If things go well, your sales could rocket and you need to make sure that you can meet demand for orders. There will be little or no sympathy if your shelf space is empty, and it will be gone to another producer in a flash. You might not get the chance again;

- Don't expect the shop to contact you to say you've sold out; they might not, so you need to keep in touch with them, build a relationship, and go in to monitor stock levels yourself from time to time or as often as you can;

- Supermarkets can be fickle. Sometimes, they will randomly stop ordering your food, or some of your range, with no notice, no apparent reason and no explanation that you can find out, and no sign of them re-ordering them again;

- Merchandising is very important in supermarkets. In other words, where in the shop your foods are located, where on the shelf they're located, how many "facings" you'll be given, and how they look on the shelf;

- Supermarkets will pay on receipt of an invoice only, and usually will only accept one invoice a month. Even if you deliver three or four times each month, you only issue one invoice. Instead, give them a delivery docket with each delivery so you both keep track. Be clear about your terms, - for example, payment is due 30 days from receipt of invoice, and then follow-up (this advice goes for all customers actually).

Supermarket multiples all compete fiercely for the top spot in terms of sales. If you can convince them that your foods can help them achieve this, then you've got a foot in the door. They all promote local food producers, and run campaigns to show just how much they're behind you. But never forget, they're not a charity, they're not a support agency, they're companies with an eye always on the bottom line. They want you only because you can help them achieve sales by attracting customers who want to buy Irish/British/Scottish etc.

In Ireland (see **Chapter 16** for the UK), the top three supermarkets are Dunnes Stores, SuperValu and Tesco, with Aldi and Lidl hot on their heels for market share.

Dunnes Stores partners with many local producers and supports producers in developing foods, especially for the Simply Better range. To find out about becoming a Simply Better producer, look at www.dunnesstoresgrocery.com/sm/delivery/rsid/258/simplybetter-producers/ or email simplybetterproducers@dunnes-stores.ie.

Musgrave Group's (www.musgravegroup.com) SuperValu and Centra stores are supplied through the Musgrave Distribution System, which is used for fresh, chilled and frozen foods. However, individual shops in this supermarket group also purchase directly from local suppliers, so try that first. SuperValu and Bord Bia run the Food Starter and Food Academy (www.supervalu.ie/real-people/food-academyprogramme/) through the LEOs (www.localenterprise.ie), which gives successful participants access to a number of local SuperValu stores with a view to gaining national sales in the longer term.

Producers who want to sell in Tesco must make their approach *via* head office in Dublin, not to local stores, and should fill in the online "Red Door" application form (talk about impersonal!) with details (www.tescoplc.com/innovation/innovationcontact/). You'll find more information here: www.tescoplc.com/contacts/suppliers/.

Lidl operates the Kick Starter programme to get small food producers on shelves in Ireland (www.lidl.ie/c/kickstart/s10020775) and Northern Ireland (www.lidl-ni.co.uk/c/kickstart/s10026058).

In Ireland, Aldi runs a National Brown Bread baking competition (www.aldi.ie/brown-bread-competition) in association with the National Ploughing Championships (www.npa.ie) and the Irish Countrywomen's Association (www.ica.ie) – the winner is stocked in stores for 12 months. For all other food producers, there is the Grow with Aldi campaign for producers in Ireland (www.aldi.ie/grow).

BWG Food Group includes Spar, Eurospar, Mace, Londis and XL (as well as a number of foodservice brands) – see www.bwg.ie.

Costcutter (www.costcutter.ie) is another franchise chain and is a supporter of Irish producers through its *Bia Éireannach* programme.

Holland & Barrett International is the largest health and wellness retailers in Europe, supplying its customers with vitamins, minerals, health supplements and specialist foods. It is interested in sourcing locally in the countries where it has stores. Check www.hollandandbarrett.com/info/supplying-holland-and-barrett/).

## Distributors, agents & wholesalers

Using a third party to bring your foods to the shops and consumers is a good option as your business grows. These come in all sorts of shapes and sizes.

Some market stallholders will sell your foods for you, although some markets won't let others sell on your behalf; some agents will sell your foods to shops they have on their route; some wholesalers will buy from you and sell it on, and some distributors will sell as well as deliver.

Whichever of these, or combination of them, you go for, make sure you are happy for them to represent you and your foods. See more about Distribution in the section below;

## Food service

This is the term used to describe all food consumed outside the home – for example, in catering, restaurants, hotels, pubs, canteens, hospitals, schools, vending machines, takeaways/on-the-go, service station forecourts and so on.

If you are able to make a quality product with your USPs clearly defined, then local restaurateurs, hotels, cafés, coffee shops and pubs who are motivated and interested in using and promoting local producers might be interested. Some chefs and restaurateurs are particularly keen to feature local producers on their menus, and may even be prepared to pay a premium, especially those who are interested in provenance and promoting local food to attract discerning diners.

Many producers rely on the food service sector for sales. However, be aware that it may not be as simple as approaching a chef (although this is always the best starting point), as some hotel chains use a central buying system such as ProcureWizard for approved suppliers.

If you decide that your foods would sell well through food service, then I urge caution. Be careful about payment arrangements. Try to agree for cash on delivery if you can with smaller outlets, or strict credit terms, and don't allow credit to build up. Payment can be slow, so plan for this in your cash-flow projections.

One of the advantages of selling to this sector is that the labelling requirements are a bit simpler. Your packaging won't need to be elaborate either. There are risks though – don't leave yourself over-reliant on a few customers; if they close, then it would be your loss too.

As well as the hospitality sector, food service includes service station forecourts, such as Applegreen (www.applegreenstores.com), Circle K (www.circlek.ie) and Maxol. 'Homegrown at Maxol' (www.maxol.ie/homegrown) is a programme that gives food producers the opportunity to be distributed across the network of Maxol stores in Ireland.

Quick service restaurants (takeaways), the travel industry (airlines and ferries), big catering companies like Aramark (www.aramark.ie), Sodexo (ie.sodexo.com) and others who operate large institutional canteens within universities and multi-nationals, public procurement for government contracts if you're large enough to supply them, all may be options for you in the future.

B2B could be another avenue, where you supply your foods as an element or ingredient into sandwich makers or companies producing salad bowls, for example.

Some distributors – such as Odaois Foods (www.odaois-foods.com), Sysco (www.syscoireland.com), Horgan's (www.horgans.com) and others – specialise in food service distribution, so it is worth talking to them to find out who and what they supply, and what they might be looking for to add to their offering.

## *Specialist, independent and artisan retailers*

It is always worth talking to independent retailers, those with less than 10 stores, who may take small quantities initially to test the local market and to get feedback.

Some butchers, bakers or fruit and veg shops may be interested in discussing terms with local producers when a product is ready for supply, provided it does not compete with their own lines.

You might have to agree to a sale or return arrangement (where you only get paid if the food sells, and you have to take back anything that doesn't sell) – this is quite common. In fact, it can be a good idea to explain to any shop owner that your products might bring in more customers, making it a win-win! It's not a bad way to start since the shop owner is not taking on any risk and so may be more inclined to accommodate you.

## *Meet the buyer*

You've managed to get a face-to-face meeting and a chance to present your foods to a supermarket or food service buyer. Well done! Whether you've just walked into a store and asked to speak to the manager or you've arranged a meeting with a buyer in head office, these opportunities do not come easily or often, so you want to make the most of it.

So, in preparation, what do you need to consider? First, ask yourself what you hope to gain from this meeting. There are no guarantees, and you really want to put your best foot forward. Buyers see a lot of suppliers and producers so you'll want to stand out for all the right reasons! They may or may not ask for a PowerPoint presentation, so check this beforehand. If you're not used to using PowerPoint or making presentation, practice, practice, practice, and maybe bring someone with you to give you a hand even just to set up.

Here are some tips:

- Get there on time, don't arrive in a fluster! Take a few seconds to gather yourself and your thoughts before you go on (I'm a big believer in some deep breathing exercise to calm the head);
- Know who you're meeting so you can ask for them by name when you arrive;
- Be prepared, practice your spiel. Make a good impression – one that they will remember;
- Tell them about yourself, your background, how you came to set up your food business;
- Talk about your foods, why they're so good, their USPs – what makes your foods so special;
- Talk about the target market – show you've done your research as regards who is your target market and what influences them to buy – what problem are you going to solve for them (for example, you can help them to meet healthy eating/convenience food/ organic/vegan requirements), and how they feel about that;
- Bring samples in packaging and some to taste;
- Be clear about the finances and your costs (don't tell them though!) and the RRP (recommended retail price) that you would suggest;

- Be willing and ready to negotiate. Know your margins and how low you can go and still be happy. It's OK to ask for a break/some time to think things over;
- Know what questions you want to ask them – it's OK to have them written down (it will show you've given this some thought);
- Know who your competitors are – why you are better/different;
- Reassure them about your ability to supply (continuity of supply is really important to retailers; no one likes an empty shelf);
- Come away with a name/names, contact details and clarity on next steps – should you send more samples? Ask them when you should follow-up/when you might hear back from them.

Knowing your costs cannot be emphasised enough and we will go into this in more detail in **Chapter 8**. You must know what wriggle room you have when it comes to negotiating prices. Many smaller shops will be happy to try your foods out on a sale or return basis to begin with.

In other words, effectively they don't buy them from you, but take a cut on whatever is sold, and you take back whatever is unsold. The retailers are in business after all and need to minimise their risk. *Top Ten Tips for Meeting the Buyer* can be downloaded free from my website www.alphaomega.ie.

Exhibitions and seminars/conferences are often very good places to meet buyers, and if possible, it is best to arrange an appointment with them beforehand if you can.

Good opportunities include:

- **Bord Bia Bloom:** Dublin every June Bank Holiday (www.bordbiabloom.com);
- **IFEX:** Belfast every two years (www.ifexexhibition.co.uk);
- **CATEX:** Dublin every other year (www.catexexhibition.com);
- *Blas na hÉireann*/**Irish Food Awards:** (www.irishfoodawards.com) final day (for finalists only);
- **Speciality Food Fair:** London each year (www.specialityandfinefoodfairs.co.uk);
- **Food & Drink Expo:** Birmingham every other year (www.foodanddrinkexpo.co.uk).

Any of these trade shows provide you with a chance to talk to buyers. Check out a list of shows and exhibitions, that I've compiled, which is available free from my shop on www.alphaomega.ie. You can check a specific show's website near the time to see who else will be exhibiting.

### Electronic data interchange (EDI)

Once you are successful in getting a listing with a supermarket, they may ask you to handle orders using an EDI system. Instead of using emails (or fax in the olden days!), orders are sent from the retailer to the producer using this method. You issue your invoice to the retailer using the agreed EDI too.

Don't be put off about this; once it is set up then it is usually fairly straightforward to use. A standard format is used (it might be called ANSI, EDIFACT, TRADACOMS or ebXML). Don't worry about it for now, your retail customer will help you set it up. You can find lots of explanations on line, but one of the best I've come across is from GS1ie (www.gs1ie.org or www.gs1uk.org), the same people who do barcoding.

## Exporting

Exporting your foods is a whole other ball-game. Some markets are very keen to source Irish-produced food, but you must not assume that all you have to do is send it off!

The UK accounts for 37% of Irish food and drink exports annually. However, since Brexit on 31 December 2020, the administrative burden of exporting to the UK is substantial. The negotiations that followed resulted in the development of the Northern Ireland Protocol, which was designed to ensure that there would be no "hard border" on the island of Ireland after Brexit. Further negotiations led to the "Windsor Framework" which includes arrangements to address issues such as goods travelling from Great Britain to Northern Ireland. To date, this has protected cross-border trade and provides producers with easy access to the export markets in Northern Ireland.

If you are interested in exporting either into Northern Ireland from the Republic, or into the Republic from Northern Ireland, then get in touch with Inter*Trade*Ireland early (www.intertradeireland.com) as it supports businesses who want to trade cross-border.

Bord Bia is tasked with assisting food and drink producers to export, but you need to be a Bord Bia client in order to qualify for its assistance. That said, they have some excellent resources you can access even if you're not a client company (see www.bordbia.ie/industry/exportassistance/).

For Irish producers, entering UK-based food awards competitions is a good way to get noticed by retailers, and vice versa. Examples include the Great Taste Awards (UK) (greattasteawards.co.uk) or the Quality Food Awards (uk.qualityfoodawards.com).

If you're a beef producer or quality butcher, then consider the World Steak Challenge (www.worldsteakchallenge.com).

Some of the supermarket multiples source foods for their shops internationally. For example:

- The SPAR International Challenger Brand Programme sources food for its stores internationally. For more information, email challenger@spar-international.com directly or see www.sparinternational.com/suppliers/;

- Lidl (USA) (www.lidl.com/suppliers) or contact the Head Office in each country you're interested in exporting to.

## Distribution

Food distribution is generally a major obstacle for start-up producers. Initially, you might resist paying someone else to distribute your foods, as this is yet another cost. Distribution is hard work, so you should try to plan your week and your route to be as efficient as possible. However, as your business grows, you will have to pay someone to do the driving, whether your employee or someone else, so you must build this cost into your price from the beginning. A rough rule of thumb is that distribution costs could be as much as 33% of the retail price.

If you work out the cost of doing it yourself, which limits your distribution reach since some days you'll be back at base making food and doing admin, against the cost of hiring someone and the potential increase in sales since they can travel further, then you will realise that it will pay off in the long run.

Options include 'wheels only' couriers who pick up and drop off, while others offer merchandising where they will stock shop shelves for you (at a cost, of course). Food wholesalers and chilled foods distributors – such as Sysco (www.syscoireland.com), Musgrave Marketplace (www.musgravemarketplace.ie) or Total Produce for fruit and veg (www.totalproduce.com) and many others – offer a variety of services. Bord Bia publishes *The Irish Foodservice Market Directory* every couple of years, and while some of the contact names might change, it's a really good place to start.

Don't assume that just because you may be small that they won't be interested in you as a customer. Distributors who have expressed interest in new niche, high quality, artisan food products include:

- Independent Irish Health Foods Ltd (www.iihealthfoods.com);
- Brandshapers (www.brandshapers.ie);
- Taste the View (www.tastetheview.ie);
- Wholefoods Wholesale (www.wholefoods.ie);
- Curran Foods (www.curranfoods.ie) and many others.

Keep an eye on the lorries delivering to your local shop and approach the driver, and talk to other producers for recommendations.

# Branding

Earlier, we talked about provenance and the importance of letting your customers know where your food is made. The next step is to promote this through your branding.

Taste Leitrim (www.tasteleitrim.com), The Boyne Valley Food Series in Meath & Louth (www.boynevalleyflavours.ie), the Yorkshire Pantry (www.theyorkshirepantry.com), Taste of Scotland (www.taste-of-scotland.com), Food NI (www.nigoodfood.com) and Welsh Food & Drink (www.welshfoodanddrink.wales) are all good examples of how regional branding has been used to promote a group of producers under one umbrella. The "Love Irish Food" brand (www.loveirishfood.ie) is an umbrella brand for various Irish-based producers, large and small.

Branding is always aligned to quality. A strong brand provides familiarity and creates an expectation in the mind of your customer about the level of quality in the product. Familiar food brands have strong associations for people, such as Siúcra (even though no sugar is produced in Ireland anymore!), the old Quinnsworth Yellow Pack (perceived low quality) or the premium ranges from supermarkets' own brands such as Dunnes Stores Simply Better (high quality).

## Branding vs labelling

What is the difference between branding and labelling? They're not the same thing at all. Food labelling is used to inform consumers of the properties of pre-packaged food, and the most important rule of labelling is that the consumer should not be misled (more about this in **Chapter 7**). A brand distinguishes your food from everyone else's. The brand conjures up an expectation in people's minds as to what your food will be like, where it comes from, who made it, how it's made, the ingredients, quality, and so on. While a label is functional and its main purpose is to provide specific information, a good label can enhance a brand also.

## Logo

Differentiation is very important so that your customer recognises your food label easily or does not mix your foods up with someone else's, and buy their product by mistake. As you may have a number of similar competitors, it is essential that your brand has a clear, marked difference. The logo should be evident and consistent on your packaging, website, adverts, social media, your email signature, everywhere! Ideally, people should recognise it immediately.

Graphic designers might advise that you should be brave and make a real statement, by having something different rather than creating a 'me too' brand. For example, take a look at Ben & Jerry's ice cream branding. This brand was developed in the 1970s, and still looks fresh and full of personality today. Brave branding offers a real opportunity to create a mark of difference between yourself and your competitors. Dare to be different! Talk to your graphic designer, be clear about what your brand stands for, what your 'brand values' are, and work with them to come up with something original.

There are lots of graphic designers out there, get Googling or ask around. Take a look at their work to see if you like it, or are all their logos a bit same-y?

## Defining your brand

The provenance, USPs and product characteristics of your food should be captured in your brand. Areas to consider when developing your brand include:

- **Core brand values:** Functional, emotional, coherence, consistency, credibility, innovation, co-operation, belief, partnership;
- **Where you see the brand going:** Your plans for growth and adding more product lines/food varieties.

It is important to remember that every element reflects the brand, whether it is your packaging, press releases, personality or communication.

If sub-branding (a 'Lite' version of your product, for example) is needed, ensure that it enhances the brand. Sub-brands often can weaken and confuse an overall brand.

A strong brand can provide competitive advantage in the marketplace. Your competitors may be trading also on quality, local, and artisan issues. Competition from large suppliers to supermarkets has to be considered, too.

Brand recognition is the extent to which a brand is recognised for its stated brand attributes or communications. Consumers will make associations with certain brands, both good and bad. Your food will need to communicate its brand along with the provenance, USPs and logo in order to earn recognition. Consistency is important so that the customer recognises the brand across a range of foods. Cadbury's does this well, so does Danone – no matter what the product, their main logo appears on the advert or label somewhere.

In developing a brand strategy for your foods, consider this example for a new healthy convenience food:

- Establish and promote its credentials as a source of high quality, nutritious, flavoursome, ready to eat foods;
- Promote the brand through social media channels in advance of launch and continue throughout launch period and thereafter;

- Position it as an important new enterprise development initiative;
- Use growing consumer recognition of the brand to stimulate ongoing product development;
- Develop marketing strategies to continually advance the brand;
- Develop distribution channels and both food service and retail market opportunities.

So how do you know if your strategy is working? You need to measure a few things, what you might call key performance indicators (KPIs) or targets. For example:

- Sales volumes, driving growth in your suppliers as well as yourself;
- Consumer recognition and awareness levels of the brand (you could do a survey);
- The number of new retail/food service/forecourt outlets secured;
- Profile of key accounts – what are sales like in the various outlets, are some worth keeping just for association? For example, I know one producer who sells very small volumes through Selfridge's Food Hall in London; it's not a big customer for them in terms of financial gain, but it's worth a lot in terms of customer perception and reputation;
- Visibility of the brand in marketing initiatives undertaken in retailers which focus on small or local producers.

## Trade marks

Trade marks are symbols (like logos and brand names) that distinguish goods and services in the marketplace. A trade mark must be distinctive for the goods and services you provide. In other words, it must be recognisable as a sign that differentiates your goods or service from someone else's. A trade mark is the means by which a business identifies its goods or services and distinguishes them from the goods and services supplied by other businesses.

A trade mark may consist of words (including personal names), designs, logos, letters, numerals or the shape of goods or of their packaging, or of other signs or indications that are capable of distinguishing the goods or services of one undertaking from those of others. Examples of familiar international food trademarks are: Kerrygold, Fairtrade, Cadbury, Coca Cola, McDonald's. Make sure you don't use someone else's registered trade mark, name or logo or it could get you into trouble!

Look at the website of the Intellectual Property Office of Ireland (www.ipoi.gov.ie/en/types-of-ip/trade-marks) or the UK Patents Office (www.gov.uk/browse/business/intellectual-property) for more information.

## Unique selling points

We've talked about this already, but honestly, you can't talk about it enough. Everyone can come up with several unique selling points (USPs) for their food; it just takes a bit of thought and effort. These USPs should be exploited in order to increase the value of your food to the trade and the consumer.

In order for the customer or consumer to be convinced to buy your food, the USPs must be clear. A USP defines a product's competitive advantage and is essential to identify what makes your food different from your competitors. These advantages must be emphasised every time you talk about your food to anyone who will listen!

## Provenance

For food businesses, it is really important that your provenance story is communicated well both on your packaging and through all other communication channels – website, social media, blog, advertising and images. Focusing on provenance and local sourcing provides food producers with an opportunity to differentiate themselves from competitors, especially large factory food producers. Food provenance is increasingly sought after by consumers, restaurateurs, food writers and journalists.

Bord Bia promotes Ireland as the Food Island in international marketing campaigns – just look at the Bord Bia channel on YouTube. The Kerrygold brand is known internationally and is associated with green fields, soft rain, grazing cows. The 'Taste of …' phrase is widely used in Ireland, Scotland and Northern Ireland. Irish whiskey producers are very good at using provenance to their advantage – see Clare Island Whiskey (www.clareislandwhiskey.ie).

Internationally, Italy and France are known for food.

A food's provenance will continue to be important, in particular for locally-produced food. This may be driven in part by the expectation that local food is fresher, but also the trend continues for shoppers to be increasingly keen to support local producers if they can.

Consumer research has found that, when you ask them, most shoppers prefer to buy local food, mainly because they want to support the local economy. The overall findings indicated that consumer demand is for authenticity, with health, naturalness and freshness being the primary motivating factors for purchase.

So, the provenance relating to your food products needs to be clearly defined. Take a look at some tourism websites for vocabulary: some of them are great at describing lush heathery mountainsides, sea spray, wild landscape and all that good stuff! A word of warning though – you can have all the provenance, Granny's recipe, three generations of farmers and whatever you like … but if your food doesn't taste good, if it's not good quality, they'll not be back.

## Protected Geographical Indicator/Protected Destination of Origin

Some foods are closely connected to where they are made and may use the name of the area as their brand. Examples include Champagne, which can only come from the Champagne region in France, made with champagne grapes; Italian Gorgonzola cheese; Welsh Lamb; Scottish Farmed Salmon or Melton Mowbray Pork Pies. In Ireland, you've got Achill Island Sea Salt, the Waterford Blaa and Connemara Hill Lamb, for example. These foods have either been awarded with PDO (Protected Destination of Origin), PGI (Protected Geographical Indicator) or GI (Geographical Indicator) status.

Product names registered as PDO are those that have the strongest links to the place in which they are made. PGI emphasises the relationship between the specific geographic region and the name of the product, where a particular quality, reputation or other characteristic is essentially attributable to its geographical origin. Geographical indication (GI) of spirit drinks protects the name of a spirit drink originating in a country, region or locality where the product's particular quality, reputation or other characteristic is essentially attributable to its geographical origin – for example, Irish Whiskey GI has been brewed, distilled and matured in Ireland since the 6th century, but the raw materials do not exclusively come from Ireland.

For information on the systems that operate in the UK, check out **Chapter 16**.

If your food or drink has close ties with a particular place, then it may be worth considering going for this accreditation – but it's a long road, not to be undertaken lightly!

## Case Study: Achill Island Sea Salt

The O'Malley family has revived the industry of salt production on Achill Island, which existed back in the 1800s. When I first met Marjorie O'Malley in 2013, and she described how they had started hand-harvesting seawater from the Atlantic Ocean to produce sea salt in open pans in their kitchen, I asked her, "Why?". She answered, "Because it's great fun, it's exciting!"… and hard work too I'm sure, but it certainly is worth it!

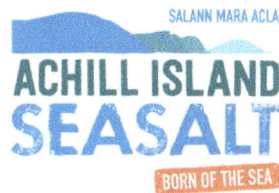

This multi-award-winning sea salt is literally the softest salt you will try; the flakes dissolve in front of your eyes. It has lower sodium than other salts and a high mineral content with over 60 naturally-occurring trace elements. As well all that, it adds really great flavour. No wonder chefs love it!

Achill Island Sea Salt (www.achillislandseasalt.ie) is produced from the clean waters of the Atlantic Ocean around Achill Island, off the West coast of Ireland. In 2023, it was awarded Protected Destination of Origin (PDO). The O'Malley's opened their Visitor Centre in 2019 and self-guided tours are available throughout the summer. The visitor centre is also home to a small gift shop which features the Achill Island Sea Salt range, Irish food products made with Achill Island Sea Salt and a number of uniquely Irish designed gifts and products. These are great examples of food tourism and partnership collaborations with other producers. Outside, you can enjoy a coffee and cake from The Salt Dock coffee truck. Achill Island Sea Salt is available in good shops all across the country.

## Food Tourism Experiences

Some places are great at attracting tourists – castles, mountains, sea, sports, walking and hiking, cycling, culture, music – you name it, they all entice tourists to an area. Food can be used to great effect too, with food trails, food-themed events, food experiences, good restaurants, food markets, local producers and so on being reason enough for some people (like me!) to visit. If you can tie your food business in with these, then you can piggy-back on their marketing activities.

In Northern Ireland, food tourism is worth over £350 million annually to the local economy; across the rest of Ireland, it's in the order of €2 billion!

Take the Greenway Cycleway in Co. Mayo in the West of Ireland – the Gourmet Greenway quickly appeared alongside it, with food producers, tearooms, restaurants and gastro pubs all letting the tourists know that they are nearby. The Wild Atlantic Way is another – with books published in no time at all, listing all the foodie places along the way. Other examples in Ireland include the Sligo Food Trail (www.sligofoodtrail.ie/food-experiences), the Old Butter Roads in Cork (www.oldbutterroads.ie), and the Burren Food Trail (www.burren.ie/visit-type/artisan-food-producers). At one point, there were close to 100 dedicated food and drink festivals held in Ireland every year, including some dedicated to seafood, street food and craft beer.

What tourists really want though is to experience the producer up close. So producers who offer interactive visitor experiences are always attractive, whether it's for a family visit on a wet day, weekend away groups looking for something different or international tourists wanting to experience something authentic. There are some considerations of course, you can't just let people wander around your (highly regulated, clean) production premises.

Many distilleries and breweries offer visits and tours:
- Ballykilcavan Brewery (www.ballykilcavan.com/tours.html);
- Bushmills Whiskey (www.bushmills.eu/distillery);
- Mescan Brewery (www.mescanbrewery.com);
- Taste Cork breweries (www.tastecork.ie/explore-cork/tastetours/craft-beer-brewery-distillery-tours);
- The Shed Distillery (www.thesheddistillery.com).

Good examples of food producers offering visitor experiences where you get to meet the producers in person include Croagh Patrick Seafoods (www.croaghpatrickseafoods.ie/tours), the Sligo Oyster Experience (www.sligooysterexperience.ie), Hazel Mountain Chocolate (www.hazelmountainchocolate.com) or the Burren Smokehouse (www.burrensmokehouse.com).

For Northern Ireland, Scotland, England and Wales, see some producer visitor experiences listed in **Chapter 16.**

## Case Study: Cashel Blue Cheese

Cashel Farmhouse Cheesemakers, producers of Cashel Blue Cheese (www.cashelbluecheese.com) which has been produced on the same 200-acre farm in Co. Tipperary for 40 years by the Grubb family. Crozier Blue, a sheep's milk blue cheese is also made, and both cheeses are multi-award winning. All of the milk used comes from within a 40 km radius of the farm, and only uses milk from grass-fed cows. In 2018, the visitor centre opened and food tourists can visit on a Tuesday (pre-booking required!) to hear about and see how the cheeses are made.

The Visitor Experience includes an in-depth cheese tasting with the cheesemakers, a 10-minute film showing how the cheese is made, the Grubb family's philosophy and history; tasting of cheese curd, young cheese, and mature cheese, sheep's cheese, and cow's cheese; a background into farmhouse cheesemaking, and of course an opportunity to purchase some quality, local cheese!

"Our Tasting Experience offers you the opportunity to visit our business, meet us, and taste the cheese on the farm where it is made and matured. It's a simple, yet very authentic food experience and it will help you get a genuine feel for how cheese makes its way from place of production in rural Ireland to your home", says Sarah Furno, joint-owner and cheese maturer, Cashel Farmhouse Cheesemakers.

## Marketing

Marketing is the assessment, creation and meeting of demand. The more detailed the market research, the sounder, more reliable the rest of your business planning will be.

You might have heard about something called the 'marketing mix', also known as the 'four Ps': Product, Place, Price and Promotion. Sometimes three more Ps are added: Process, Physical Evidence and People. All of these go towards developing your approach to marketing. So many producers I know overlook the importance of planning for marketing activities, and don't budget for them. You really must do both – plan and budget.

Your marketing plan usually looks at all the things we've talked about in the previous chapters and pulls them together, including:

- **Business profile:**
  - o Organisational structure – who does what, who is in charge;
  - o Description of your range of foods or drinks;
- **Situation analysis:**
  - o Internal Factors – Strengths, Weaknesses, Opportunities and Threats (SWOT analysis);
  - o External Factors – Political, Economic, Social, Technological, Legislative and Environmental (PESTLE analysis);
  - o Consumer trends;
  - o Competitors;
- **Market segmentation:**
  - o Target market;
  - o Consumer analysis;
  - o Market size;
  - o Route to market – different routes need different approaches;
  - o Demographics;
- **Marketing objectives:**
  - o Market share objectives – what % of the market are you after?
  - o Profit objectives – what profit level are you looking for?
  - o Increasing brand awareness;
- **Marketing communications:**

- o  Exhibitions, consumer food fairs and events, trade shows;
- o  Awards and competitions you plan to enter (see below);
- **Promotions:**
  - o  Objectives – more shops, more sales (always!);
  - o  Activities – campaigns, offers, meetings and so on;
  - o  Examples: Buy One, Get One Free (BOGOF), Multi-buys (3 for 2), Extra % free, on pack offers, in-store tastings (retailers LOVE these!), in-store recipe leaflets, social media campaigns....

We will not consider marketing any further here, since it's a huge topic in its own right, but you really must recognise its importance and look out for training courses or marketing mentors in your area to help you if necessary. I will give you two tips, though:

- Put together a marketing calendar – a list of marketing activities and when you will do them, how much they will cost you (you must put aside some money for marketing);
- Promotions planning – when you will put foods on special offer.

I've put examples of both of these as free downloads on www.alphaomega.ie.

## Social Media Marketing

Research has shown that the average social media user logs into about seven platforms each month. Seven. Not spending time on social media or digital marketing as part of your marketing activities is like saying working from home or hybrid working would never take off!

Facebook, X (formerly Twitter), Instagram, Snapchat, TikTok, YouTube and the rest are all free to use, other than the cost of your time. They are updated so often though, it can be hard to keep up. Compared to other media, it's a cheap and effective way to spread the word about your business, your new products, your provenance and your brand – everything you want to tell the world about you, your food and your business. Your posts may not be seen unless you spend money on adverts aimed at your target market. And then there's the cost of your time...

As with looking at your target market for your foods, consider your target market when deciding which social media channels to use. For example, younger audiences tend to use Snapchat and TikTok more than anything else (including SMS) and hardly ever use Facebook.

Social media marketing is not something you do sitting on the couch at night while half-watching TV. It takes planning. Planning your posts should be structured, posting three or four times per week on all platforms that you use. You will need to adjust your posts and images depending on where you plan to put them It is important to be consistent in your messaging and regular with frequent updates. Video works really well and you'll get used to it!

Social media marketing is a task, a job for someone. If you feel it's not for you, if you don't have time or skills or the inclination, then get someone else to do it for you or get some training, but don't ignore it.

Also consider becoming familiar with Generative AI for digital marketing and how to use ChatGPT and other AI (artificial intelligence) business tools for content creation for your social media marketing. You may find it useful for your business in the future.

You should register your business on your chosen social media channel as soon as you can, as many names are already taken. Check out www.namecheck.com to see if yours is available.

If you need help getting to grips with social media or ChatGPT/AI, then contact your Local Enterprise Office (www.localenterprise.ie) or Council as they're always running courses on Social Media for Business and the like. I've listed some useful books in **Chapter 17**.

## Food Awards & Competitions

Entering your food product into any of the many food awards and competitions is a great way to get free promotion and PR for you and your food business. You don't have to be nominated, you can (and should) enter yourself.

The big ones in Ireland for food producers are the *Blas na hÉireann*/National Irish Food Awards (www.irishfoodawards.com) and the IQFAs (www.irish.qualityfoodawards.com). Then there are awards run by Good Food Ireland (www.goodfoodireland.ie), as well as an annual award from the Irish Food Writers Guild (www.irishfoodwritersguild.ie/food-awards). Euro-toques also has awards, with details of past winners available on www.euro-toques.ie.

Local Enterprise Offices run the National Enterprise Awards competition annually, although this is not limited to food producers; so does the Small Firms Association (www.sfa.ie); and many of the banks sponsor awards too and there are many others.

In the UK, it's the Great Taste Awards run by the Guild of Fine Food (www.greattasteawards.co.uk), and these are open to food producers from Ireland also, as well as the Quality Food Awards (uk.qualityfoodawards.com) among many others.

There are many specialist awards too including the British Cheese Awards (www.britishcheeseawards.com) or for free-from, frozen food, awards for vegan food, for drinks, best chilli, best ethnic foods, best Organic, best Private label, for food innovation, you name it! If you get shortlisted, even if you don't win, it's great for your business/product profile and it's all free advertising!

The focus in this section is on awards for food and drink producers; however there are lots of other awards competitions for the hospitality sector, including Street Food (www.europeanstreetfood.com/2023-awards).

# 7

# LABELLING, NUTRITION CLAIMS & ALLERGENS

## Food Labelling

Food labelling is used to tell consumers what is in their food. If your food is in a packet, bag, carton, jar or bottle when it leaves your kitchen (pre-packed), then it must have a label on it. This applies to pre-packed foods whether sold in shops or online ('distance selling'), or anywhere.

The legislation that covers all food labelling is called Food Information to Consumers (FIC). The most important rule of labelling is that the consumer should not be misled. The label cannot make any claims about a food's ability to prevent, treat or cure a human illness!

'Labelling' means any words, trademarks, brand name, pictures or symbols relating to the food and placed anywhere relating to the food. The information on the label must be easy to understand, be clearly legible; it must also be indelible, easy-to-see and not obscured in any way. Food products, including food imports sold in Ireland, which must be labelled in English (with optional labelling in Irish or another language as well as, but not instead of, English).

Generally, if food is sold loose, like in a bakery, or deli counter or market stall and you only put it into a bag when you're handing it over to the customer, then it doesn't need a label. However, legislation that applies to all unwrapped or non-prepacked foods, specifically in relation to allergens, requires all food businesses including restaurants, delis, canteens, pubs, takeaways and retail outlets providing non-prepacked foods, such as unwrapped foods or meals, to indicate to consumers the use of any of the 14 listed allergenic ingredients in the production or preparation of the food. We talk more about allergens below.

There is specific additional labelling legislation for:

- Meat from pigs, sheep, goats, poultry;
- Mincemeat;
- Sausage casings;
- Defrosted foods;
- Irradiated foods;
- Substituted ingredients (where the consumer would make an assumption about what is in your food);
- Beef;
- Country of Origin for honey, olive oil, fruit and vegetables, fish;
- Products with meat as an ingredient;
- Jams, jellies and marmalades (see **Chapter 11**);
- Foods containing quinine or caffeine;
- Food supplements;
- Alcoholic beverages;
- Additives.

Some of these are covered below. For the others, ask your EHO, for example, or look them up on www.fsai.ie (or read *Regulation EU 1169/2011)*, www.food.gov.uk or www.foodstandards.gov.scot.

There is an exception to the rule for small packages or containers where the largest surface is less than 10cm² (such as chocolate wedding favours) – in this case, only the name of the food, the net quantity, date of minimum durability and any allergens, (for example, the words 'contains peanuts') are required.

There are requirements about the minimum font size, which specifies a font size where the height of the letter x is equal to or greater than 1.2mm (your graphic designer will know what this means). And, in the case of packaging or containers, the largest surface of which has an area of less than 80cm², the x-height of the font size must be equal to or greater than 0.9mm.

## What Must Appear on the Label?

There is a mountain of legislation about food labelling. However, you should start with general labelling legislation, which says that the following must appear on the label:

1. Name of the food;
2. List of ingredients;
3. Allergens must be indicated *within* the list of ingredients;
4. Quantity of certain ingredients (called QUID);
5. Net quantity;
6. Date of minimum durability – Best Before or Use By dates;
7. Special storage instructions or conditions of use;
8. Name or business name and address of the producer, manufacturer, packager, seller or importer within the EU;
9. Country of Origin or Place of Provenance (see above);
10. Instructions for use, if necessary;
11. Beverages with more than 1.2% alcohol by volume must declare their actual alcoholic strength;
12. Nutrition Declaration.

There are many exceptions and special cases for all elements of the labelling legislation. If your food has been freeze-dried or defrosted or smoked or concentrated some other treatment, that has to be declared too. What is described above is for food in general. For any specifics relating to *your* food, it's a good idea to check your labels with your EHO/Inspector.

### Name of the food

This means its legal name, such as 'chocolate' or 'butter', 'milk' or 'raw milk' as these are defined in la;, its customary name, say 'shepherd's pie', 'fish fingers' or 'Yorkshire pudding'; or the name that describes what it actually is, like 'vegetable soup'. If you call your product something vague like 'Mary's Winter Casserole', then must add a line so that customers know exactly what it is – like this:

**Mary's Winter Casserole**
*Beef and vegetables in gravy*

## List of ingredients

If your food contains two or more ingredients, then they should be listed in descending order of quantity, starting with the ingredient with the largest amount in your recipe. In addition:

- Products requiring reconstitution may be listed as dehydrated or rehydrated;

- If you use additives, then you can either use the E number alone or the name, or both, as you prefer – for example, 'thickener (E412)', 'thickener (Guar Gum)' or 'thickener (E412/Guar Gum)';

- For compound ingredients (ingredients that have more than one component themselves, such as the pastry in a fruit pie or mayonnaise in coleslaw), you must list their ingredients separately too unless they are less than 2% of the final product – and there are some other exceptions;

- The amount of added water need not be listed as an ingredient if it is less than 5% by weight of the finished product;

- If you are using water for ingredient reconstitution (in other words, using it to reconstitute dry ingredients before adding them into your sausage mixture, for example) or if the water is not going to be eaten (like tuna or olives in brine), then you do not have to declare it as an ingredient;

- If your food contains certain allergens (ingredients that are scientifically proven to cause an allergic reaction), then you must highlight them within the ingredients list, see below.

## Allergens

The way that certain allergens are required to be listed on labels is described specifically in the legislation (Annex II of *Directive EU 1169/2011*).

The allergens that must be listed are:

1. Cereals containing gluten, namely: wheat (such as spelt and khorasan wheat), rye, barley and oats – allergen here means the name of the cereal – for example, 'wheat' and not 'gluten';

2. Crustaceans (crabs, lobsters, crayfish, shrimp);

3. Eggs;

4. Fish;

5. Peanuts;

6. Soybeans;

7. Milk;

8. Nuts, namely: almonds, hazelnuts, walnuts, cashews, pecan nuts, Brazil nuts, pistachio nuts, macadamia or Queensland nuts – allergen here means the name of the nut – for example, 'pistachio nut' and not 'nut';

9. Celery;

10. Mustard;

11. Sesame seeds;

12. Sulphur dioxide and sulphites at concentrations of more than 10mg/kg or 10mg/L;

13. Lupin (lupin flour or lupin seeds can be used in baking);

14. Molluscs (snails, clams, oysters, octopus, squid).

For example:

| INGREDIENTS |
|---|
| Water, Carrots, Onions, Red lentils (4.5%), Potato, Cauliflower, Leeks, Peas, Cornflour, **Wheat flour**, **Cream (milk)**, Yeast extract, Concentrated tomato paste, Garlic, Sugar, **Celery seed**, Sunflower oil, Herbs and Spices, White pepper, Parsley. |
| **ALLERGY ADVICE** |
| For Allergens, see ingredients in **bold.** |

That's quite a list! So, if you are unsure, ask for help from your EHO or Inspector or other qualified nutrition or food science and technology expert or from the FSAI, FSA or Food Standards Scotland.

## Quantity of certain ingredients

This is called QUID, short for 'quantitative ingredient declaration'. What it means is that, in certain instances, the percentage of specific ingredients is declared on a label if the name of the food implies that the food contains a specific ingredient – for example:

- Irish Stew – declare % meat;
- Fish Fingers – declare % fish;
- Chilli con Carne – declare % beef;
- "with cheese topping" – declare % cheese;
- Leek and Potato Soup – declare % leek and % potato.

The panel below is an example for a sachet of Italian tomato pasta sauce. The ingredients list must declare the various ingredients mentioned in its name. In this case, the percentage of tomatoes and tomato purée are given.

| **INGREDIENTS** |
| --- |
| Tomatoes (51%), Onions, Olive oil, Tomato purée (4%), Sugar, Peppers, White wine vinegar, Spring onions, Chillies, Sea salt, Cracked black pepper, Garlic. |

The next panel shows the labelling for a tub of hummus, whose legal name is 'Greek-style chickpea and sesame seed paste dip with lemon juice and garlic'. Since the consumer expects hummus to contain chickpeas among other things, the ingredients list must declare the percentage of these used. It was considered unnecessary to declare the percentage of the various types of nuts:

| **Lemon and Garlic Hummus** |
| --- |
| Greek-style Chickpea and Sesame Seed Dip, with Lemon Juice and Garlic |
| INGREDIENTS: Cooked chickpeas (43%) [chickpeas, water], Rapeseed oil, **Sesame seed** paste (16%), Water, Concentrated lemon juice (3%), Garlic purée, Salt, Preservative (Potassium sorbate) |
| For allergy advice, see ingredients **highlighted in bold.** |

An organic label might include an ingredients list along these lines:

| **Organic Hummus** |
| :---: |
| A Rich and Creamy Blend of Organic Chickpeas, Tahini, Garlic and Lemon Juice |
| INGREDIENTS: Organic cooked chickpeas (56%), Water, Organic sunflower oil, Organic tahini paste (11%) (crushed **sesame seeds**), Organic lemon concentrate (3%), Organic garlic (2%), Salt. |

QUID is not required if the percentage declaration is covered by other legislation, like in the case of jam (see below). However, you might like to declare all the vegetable percentages if you are producing a mixed vegetable soup, for example, because it's a good way of showing your customers all the tasty ingredients that are in it!

## Net quantity

The net quantity means the weight or volume of the food without its packaging. If your food is packed in liquid (say mozzarella cheese or jars of tuna), then it's the drained weight that should be declared – that is, just the food, not the water or oil that it's packed in. Some products are exempt from weight marking, such as packets that weigh less than less than 5g in weight or 5ml in volume (except spices and herbs).

In Ireland and the UK, you don't have to show the weight of foods that are sold by number or that are weighed out in front of the consumer. For example, two bread rolls that can easily be seen through the packaging, or if sweets or nuts are weighed out, or on multipacks where you can state, say, 5 x 50g, where the individual unit weighs 50g.

The average system of weight control is denoted by the 'e' mark. What this means in effect is that the weight or volume of the food is an average weight or volume. Using the 'e' mark is voluntary, but it is very useful if you're planning to export your foods within Europe.

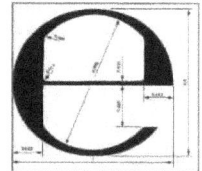

For example, let's say your pre-packed bag of buns has a stated weight on the label of 250g. Then if you weighed 10 bags of buns, on average, each bag would have to weigh 250g, even if some were a little bit more and some a little bit less. If you want to start getting into the complexities as to how much a 'little bit' actually means, you can check out the legislation in detail (*EC Packaged Goods (Quantity Control) Act, 1980* and *Packaged Goods (Quantity Control) Act, 1981*).

## Date of minimum durability

The difference between Best Before and Use By dates was covered in the Shelf Life section of **Chapter 5**. As described by *safe*food (www.safefood.eu), Best Before is a *guideline* and Use By is a *deadline*.

The key difference is that Use By is for perishable foods that might cause food poisoning or illness because they are likely to contain unacceptable levels of bacteria or other microbes after that date.

Generally, foods that must be kept in the fridge to maintain their safety rather than their quality, and those that have a relatively short shelf life after they have been made, require a Use By date – for example, ready-to-eat foods or foods that must be cooked or reheated before eating, such as meat, fish, poultry, and eggs as well as some dairy products. It is illegal to sell food after its Use By date has passed.

Frozen foods have a Best Before date. Again, there are some exceptions, so check out what's right for your food.

## Special storage instructions and/or conditions of use

If the food must be kept in the fridge or in a cool dry place in order to maintain its shelf life, then you need to put this message on the label to tell the consumer what they have to do when they get the food home. You also should mention how long to keep the pack once it has been opened, or whether they need to store it in the fridge once opened.

## Name or business name and address of the food business (manufacturer, packager, seller or importer)

The contact details must be precise enough so that, in the event of a customer complaint, the person making the complaint can contact you. You should use a postal address, somewhere a letter can reach you. A website address or phone number is not acceptable on their own.

It is very important to note that, even if you outsource your production to someone else (a third party), it is YOUR name and address that should be on the label, not theirs.

## Country of origin or place of provenance

The place of provenance is required if its absence might significantly mislead the consumer. For example, if you make 'Italian sausage', but you make it in Cork, or you make Brie cheese (typically a French cheese) in Tipperary. If you do, then make it clear – for example, "Tipperary Brie". It needs to be clear on the label where the food was made. As long as the consumer doesn't think it came from some place it didn't, then that's fine.

The Country of Origin can be indicated on the label by simply stating it in words, using an image (map or scene), or symbol (for example, a flag), or through words/terms or colours/designs that refer to a geographical origin.

Some categories of food are obliged by law to indicate the country of origin (beef, fruit and vegetables, honey, olive oil, fish). Beef, pig meat, sheep meat, goat and poultry products must also have details of where the animal was born, reared and slaughtered.

If the country of origin of the food product is not the same as the origin of the primary (main) ingredient, then the origin of the primary ingredient must also be given. For example, where the origin of a beef casserole is declared as Irish on the label but the beef is not Irish, then you must also give the origin of the beef on the label. Otherwise, the consumer might be confused and assume, incorrectly, that the beef is Irish.

The legislation can be a bit tricky, so it is best to check it out thoroughly (*Regulation EU 1337/2013*).

By the way, restaurants, cafés or anywhere that food is sold to a consumer must show the country of origin on the menu for foods including any meat, fish or seafood products.

## Instructions for use

This is where you tell the customer how to prepare, cook or reheat the food, whether it's suitable for frying or baking, or whether it should be thawed before use, for example.

## Alcoholic drinks

Beverages with more than 1.2% alcohol by volume must declare their actual alcoholic strength.

# Nutrition Labelling

When you read a label and see a table that lists the Energy (kJ or Cal), Fat, Carbohydrate, Protein, and Salt in the product, this is called 'nutrition labelling'. In December 2016, nutrition information became mandatory for most pre-packaged foods.

There are some exemptions for food producers making small quantities (defined as 250kg or litres of products per week, or 13,000kg or litres of products per year, or 500 units per week, or 26,000 units per year) of products to the final consumer or to local (<100km away from where you're making it) retail establishments. There are different rules for the UK, so check out **Chapter 16** for details.

However, even before it became a legal requirement, many producers chose to label their foods with nutrition information to enable consumers to make more informed choices about the nutrition characteristics of the food. It costs money to analyse and list the various nutrients, and to print up the labels, so don't do this until you are sure that you won't be changing the recipe any time soon.

So how do you work out the nutritional analysis figures? There are three ways:

- Send the food off to a lab for analysis;
- Work it out by hand using your recipe and the tables of figures for the various ingredients from McCance & Widdowson's book, *The Composition of Foods*;
- Use special nutritional analysis software to work it out (NutriCalc, Capterra, MicroDiet , Nutritics or NutritionalPro are some examples and there are plenty of others).

Any of these methods is acceptable. The second option is laborious, and it depends on how much you like getting stuck into calculations and formulae. You might find it cheaper to buy the software for a year than getting your foods tested, depending on how many products you have to test. It is entirely up to you to choose the method.

The nutrients must be declared per 100g or per 100ml – and you must list them in this order:

| Mandatory Information/ 100g or 100ml | Supplementary Information (if desired) |
|---|---|
| Energy (kJ/kcal) | |
| Fat of which Saturates | of which Monounsaturates of which Polyunsaturates |
| Carbohydrate of which Sugars | of which Polyols of which Starch |
| | Fibre |
| Protein | |
| Salt | |
| | Vitamins and Minerals (% RI) |
| **You MUST list all of these.** | **You MAY include all of these if you wish (either all or none).** |

If you wish, you can also add in another column to show the nutrition information *per portion*. For example, per biscuit, per bar, per sandwich. This is useful for the consumer who may find it tricky to work it out for themselves, but it's not a legal requirement.

Front-of-pack labelling is also voluntary – you can show the Energy on its own or the Energy, Fat, Saturates, Sugar and Salt (all of these). Having said that, many of the major supermarkets and many food manufacturers provide this information anyway, and use the government's recommended format – red, amber, green colour-coding and percentage reference intakes (RIs) – or as you may better recognise it – traffic light labelling.

On the next page is an example of the elements of a simple compliant label that you could give to a graphic designer to work with.

Note that the following items must appear in the same field of vision on the label:

- Name;
- Net quantity;
- Actual alcohol content (if over 1.2% alcohol by volume).

| **Fresh Tomato and Basil Soup** |
|---|
| *Ingredients: Potato, Tomato (25%), Onion, Vegetable stock, **Celery**, Basil (2%).*<br><br>*Use by: dd/mm/yyyy*<br>Keep refrigerated.<br>Once opened, use within 2 days or before Use By date if sooner.<br><br>*Monnie's Fine Foods, Foodville, Co. Leitrim*<br>225g |

## Nutrition & health claims

If you claim that your food is high or low in fat or salt or calories or fibre, for example, then you have to be able to stand over this claim. The following are some examples of 'nutrition claims' that are defined in the legislation:

- Reduced fat: 30% reduction compared with standard product;
- Low fat: Maximum of 3g/100g per product;
- Reduced calories: 30% reduction compared to standard product;
- Low calories: Maximum 167Kj (40Kcal) per product.

For more about nutrition claims, contact the FSAI or FSA.

The other type of claim that is sometimes made is a 'health claim' (covered under *Regulation EC 1924/2006*). This is any claim that states, suggests or implies that a relationship exists between a food (or one of its constituents) and health, such as reducing the risk of disease or referring to children's development and health (for example, 'calcium is good for children's growth'). This is acceptable under law, provided there is scientific data to prove it (which can be difficult and expensive) or that the relationship has been around for so long that consumers understand it (for example, everyone knows that fibre is good for your digestion).

The term 'probiotic', refers to probiotic bacteria, and when used on a food label, is considered to be a health claim. However, there are no proven health claims registered with the EU at the moment and that includes probiotics.

By the way, you cannot use the word 'live' on dairy products either, without checking that your foods meet the specific criteria in *Regulation EC 1924/2006*. So, check it out and get your foods tested before you start making any claims on the label.

Also, any health claim that states, suggests or implies that eating a particular food significantly reduces a risk factor in the development of human disease is prohibited! For more information, check out www.food.ec.europa.eu/safety/labelling-and-nutrition/nutrition-and-health-claims_en/.

### Distance Selling

If you sell food through an e-commerce website or online shop, the same labelling requirements apply as if you were selling it through a physical shop.

Since the customer cannot examine the packaging before they purchase, or they can't hold it in their hand, then you must provide access to all of the mandatory food information before they complete their purchase. This mandatory information includes all information that must be given to the consumer, not just that on the label, and must be available before the online purchase is concluded.

The same goes for non-prepacked foods.

All you need to do is to provide it on your website where your customer can see it all before they finalise their order.

## Organic Labelling

There are particular requirements for the labelling of organic products in the EU as per *Regulation (EC) 834/2007*). In Ireland, information is available from one of two approved certification bodies (see **Chapter 16** for UK information):

- Irish Organic Farmers & Growers Association (www.iofga.org);
- Organic Trust (www.organic-trust.org).

Organic labelling includes requirements for displaying the organic certification license number, the symbol of the particular certification body with whom you are registered, the phrase 'Certified Organic', as well as all the standard stuff above.

It is important to note that, just because the food is organic, you are not permitted to claim it is superior. If you use organic ingredients, then you can only apply for organic certification for your finished food if the ingredients of agricultural origin make up:

- Minimum of 95% by weight of the foodstuff; and
- Maximum of 5% by weight of total is from the permitted nonorganically produced ingredient list.

Sometimes, you see labels declaring 'made using organic ingredients'. What this means usually is that, while the food producer themselves is not organic-certified, they buy organic-certified ingredients and use them in their foods.

In other cases, where 70% to 95% of the ingredients of agricultural origin in the foodstuff are organic, then although the product itself cannot be labelled as organic, you can indicate that it does contain some organic ingredients. Check the legislation to ensure you comply with the restrictions though.

The other thing to know is that *Regulation EU 2018/848* limits the addition of vitamins and minerals to organic products.

## Gluten-free Labelling

Just because you use Tritamyl flour in your foods doesn't mean you can label them as being 'gluten-free'. By law, food labelled 'gluten-free' must contain less than 20mg gluten/kg (< 20 parts per million (ppm)). This level is suitable for the most sensitive of coeliacs. The specific legislation is *EU 828/2014*.

So, if you bake bread and you want to label it as gluten-free, then you must be absolutely sure that it contains less than 20mg gluten/kg. It's not just a matter of complying with the legislation for your own sake, but it could have a detrimental health implication for a person with coeliac disease if it doesn't comply. These are legal terms, not to be taken lightly!

'Wheat-free' does not mean that the product is gluten-free. The product may contain other gluten-containing cereals, such as spelt.

Sometimes you may see on a package 'Made in a factory handling gluten' or 'May contain gluten'. When you see this statement, the manufacturer has decided that there is a cross-contamination risk within the manufacturing process.

### Crossed Grain symbol European licensing system

The Crossed Grain symbol is nationally and internationally recognised by those who need to follow a gluten-free diet as it is promoted by coeliac organisations worldwide. The symbol is synonymous with gluten-free and represents a sign of safety and integrity. In an environment where food labels and legislative changes can be bewildering for someone on a gluten-free diet, the crossed grain symbol has been proven to provide consumers a quick reference point when out shopping and faced with the uncertainty on the gluten-free status of a product.

*Source: www.coeliac.ie*

To use the Crossed Grain symbol, your products must meet a range of criteria to ensure that they are gluten-free, both in terms of the ingredients and the production process. Obtaining a Crossed Grain licence for your product costs from €500 *pa*, depending on the turnover of your gluten-free products. The certification lasts for a full year from the date that the certification is taken out.

For information on licencing the Crossed Grain symbol or on how you can better cater to the gluten-free consumer, contact the Coeliac Society of Ireland (www.coeliac.ie) or Coeliac UK (www.coeliac.org.uk).

## Promotional & Other Labels

Apart from the labelling requirements covered by legislation, what other labels might you put on your food?

Promotional labels like 'buy one, get one free', competition alerts to let the buyer know that they are in with a chance of winning something, awards labels shouting about your recent successes, flash labels to point out that your food is 'yeast-free' are some examples.

There is nothing from stopping you putting on any or all of these except that the legal labels have to take priority. Just be careful that it all doesn't get very crowded and unattractive-looking.

# 8

# MAKING & MANAGING MONEY

You don't necessarily need thousands of euros or pounds to start a small food business, though you may need to invest in equipment and premises. The main thing in starting and maintaining a successful food business is a drive and a passion for what you are doing, and a willingness to work hard. However, you need to be sure that, having put in all the effort, you see some rewards – preferably monetary!

## Pricing & Margins

When you hear people talking about pricing models and margins, what do they mean?

| Cost to Produce | + | Profit Margin (mark-up) | = | Selling Price |
|---|---|---|---|---|

'Pricing' is the total of what it actually costs you to make the product, plus a margin for your profit.

Premium pricing is where your customer is willing to pay extra for something of special value to them. Consumers know that they usually get what they pay for, so cheap food implies poor quality and they expect to pay a bit more for artisan, good quality food.

'Margin' is the slice (or slices) that everyone in the supply chain takes – for example:

- You (the producer) make the product for €2 total (including all your costs);
- The distributor, who transfers the product from you to the retailer, charged 50c – which you have to pay before it is sold to the shop for €3.50 (giving you a €1 profit margin);
- The retailer adds on their own margin of €1.00;
- The customer buys the food for €4.50.

```
        ┌─────────────────────────┐
        │   You make the food     │
        │      for €2.00          │
        └─────────────────────────┘
                    ▼
        ┌─────────────────────────┐
        │  Distributor charges    │
        │        €0.50            │
        └─────────────────────────┘
                    ▼
        ┌─────────────────────────┐
        │   You sell to the       │
        │  retailer for €3.50     │
        └─────────────────────────┘
                    ▼
        ┌─────────────────────────┐
        │     Retails to          │
        │ consumer for €4.50      │
        └─────────────────────────┘
```

It might seem to make sense initially to cut out the distributor so that you, the producer, can get the full retail price. When you are just starting out, you'll probably find that you have no choice, as you might not have the cash to pay a distributor. However, as you get busy, as production volumes increase and you're selling to more shops, then you will find it more time- and cost-effective to have someone else to distribute and sell your foods – even though this means you receive less revenue for each sale. We talked about this in **Chapter 6**.

The difficulty is in knowing what margin a shop or supermarket will want or accept; often this comes down to hard-nosed negotiations. The bigger supermarkets generally have a set margin they apply, and it could be anything from 25% to 45%, and you might not have much say in that. Smaller shops may operate on a sale or return basis, so you only get paid if the product is sold.

Regardless of where you sell, look at what your competitors are selling their products for and then you can work around that price as a starting point for cost/margin calculations.

No matter what, you must know your own costs, your absolute minimum that you will accept from the retailer before you start negotiating. What you don't want is to sell to them at too low a price, that gives you very little margin. If your costs go up, say ingredients or electricity prices, then your own margin will be squeezed too much.

Know. Your. Costs!!

## Costs

The costs that you must consider include some or all of the following:

- **Fixed Costs:**
  - Overheads – for example, rent, electricity;
  - Online selling costs, in addition to website development costs, domain registration;
  - Equipment (knives, scales, mincing equipment, cash till, etc.);
  - Stall set-up costs, if you plan to sell at Farmers' or Country markets or at events/shows, including the stall itself, tables, canopies, banners, signs, etc.;
- **Variable Costs:**
  - Ingredients;
  - Labour costs;
  - Packaging;
  - Disposables: Food safety costs, including the cost of aprons, gloves, hairnets, fridges, temperature probes, cloths, detergents, soaps, towels, waste containers and so on;
  - Distribution costs – paying a distributor/courier/wholesaler or van driver;
  - Returns: Food that comes back unsold from the retailer.

Some costs are one-off or occasional (for example, training, equipment or vehicle), some are more routine (for example, training costs – food hygiene, social media, finance; or vehicle costs, including a food trailer or refrigerated van if needed).

You'll also hear phrases including Direct (for example, ingredients, packaging, production staff costs) and Indirect (for example, marketing, insurance, rent and financial services) costs. It's good to get familiar with the terminologies when you're running your own business, so a general Start Your Own Business course might be useful.

## *Recipe cost calculation*

| CHOCOLATE CAKE | A<br>Weight (g) | B<br>Cost/weight used € |
|---|---|---|
| Butter | 175 | 0.84 |
| Chocolate | 100 | 1.11 |
| Flour | 200 | 0.25 |
| Baking powder | 5 | 0.02 |
| Bicarbonate of soda | 5 | 0.02 |
| Ground almonds | 100 | 1.05 |
| Dark brown sugar | 275 | 1.60 |
| 3 Eggs (1 egg = 60g) | 180 | 0.85 |
| Buttermilk | 150 | 0.12 |
| *ICING* | | |
| Chocolate | 90 | 1.00 |
| Butter | 40 | 0.19 |
| Double cream | 150 | 0.95 |
| **Total Ingredients Costs** | | **8.00** |
| Electricity | | 0.50 |
| Labour | | 6.50 |
| Packaging | | 2.00 |
| **TOTAL COST TO MAKE** | | **17.00** |
| Add on distribution costs | | 1.00 |
| Add on your margin | | 2.00 |
| **SELLING PRICE (direct sales)** | | **20.00** |
| Add on retailer's margin | | 5.00 |
| **SELLING PRICE (indirect sales)** | | **25.00** |

*Note:* **You must include payment for your labour.** The majority of small food producers and indeed small businesses starting up forget this. But if you can't pay yourself, then you're not in business!

Now ask yourself: Will a customer pay €25 for a chocolate cake? The answer depends on why they are buying it. If it is a large cake for a special occasion, then the answer is "Probably", otherwise it's more likely to be, "No".

As you get into the swing of your business, you may be able to source the same ingredients more cheaply. Or you may be able to substitute cheaper ingredients without compromising the quality.

## Running costs per day for a food stall

You should know your outlays before you even sell one loaf/jar/tub of anything at a market. Some markets charge more than others for the pitch, but this table will give you an idea of the costs.

| Food Stall Costs | | € |
|---|---|---|
| **Rent of stall** | Per day | 25 |
| **Labour** | 8 hours/day /1 person @ €12.70/hr (minimum wage/Ireland/2024) | 102 |
| **Insurance** | Estimate per week | 5 |
| **Fuel** | For travel to/from the market | 5 |
| **TOTAL COST per day before you sell anything!** | | **137** |

# Projected Income

So how much are you hoping to earn? When I mentor new food businesses, I always suggest that they start with their aspirational target annual income, whether it's replacing income from a current job or a target for where they want to get to.

So, let's say you want to earn €20,000 per year from baking chocolate cakes. In the example above, you're paying yourself €6.50 per cake, so that's 3,076 cakes per year you need to be selling! That's 10 cakes a day, six days a week!

Looking at it another way, if you want the business to turn over (in other words, bring in) €40,000 per year you need to make 2,222 cakes per year just to bring in €40,000 so that you can pay yourself €14,400.

If you want to pay yourself double that, or €28,800 per year, then charge more per cake, another €6.50 per cake in fact, but you'll still need to make over 2,000 cakes per year. Not really likely, is it?

My advice in this case would be to charge more per cake, let's say €40, and in that way you can increase your income and at the same time reduce the number of cakes you have to make.

Another way to project your income and give you targets to aim for at the same time, is to set out how many of which products you want to sell to what customers/shops – in a table like the one below.

| Projected/Desired Sales by Shop or Product Customer/Product | | | | | | TOTAL € |
|---|---|---|---|---|---|---|
| | A | B | C | D | E | |
| January | | | | | | |
| February | | | | | | |
| March | | | | | | |
| April | | | | | | |
| May | | | | | | |
| June | | | | | | |
| July | | | | | | |
| August | | | | | | |
| September | | | | | | |
| October | | | | | | |
| November | | | | | | |
| December | | | | | | |
| **ANNUAL TOTAL** | | | | | | |

## Sources of Finance & Funding

Local Enterprise Offices (LEOs) (www.localenterprise.ie), Local Authorities, County Councils and the Rural Development Partnerships (LEADER companies) (www.nationalruralnetwork.ie/ www.leaderprogramme.org.uk) or Local Action Groups (UK) may help you with funding for feasibility studies, training (often free) or equipment. In addition, they usually offer access to experienced mentors with specialisms in food, finance and business start-up, often for free, but certainly for a small percentage of the actual cost. The LEOs also may provide funding for attendance at trade shows.

Enterprise Ireland and Invest Northern Ireland have Innovation Voucher schemes (www.enterprise-ireland.com/en/supports/ innovation-voucher/ or www.investni.com/support-for-business/ innovation-vouchers/), open to food businesses registered as companies. Sole traders are generally not eligible but sometimes the scheme is opened to sole traders or artisan producers, so keep an eye out for this opportunity. The UK has a similar scheme (www.ukinnovationhub.ukri.org/offerings/innovation-vouchers/).

The New Frontiers programme (www.newfrontiers.ie) is Ireland's national entrepreneur development programme, funded by Enterprise Ireland and delivered at a local level by the Technological Universities and some Universities.

Inter*Trade*Ireland (www.intertradeireland.com) runs the SeedCorn business plan competition each year for start-up and early stage businesses, as well as offering other funding for sales and marketing (Acumen programme) and for innovation (Innovation Boost programme), once you're established and trading for a couple of years. The Elevate programme helps to develop cross-border sales across the island.

The Food Works programme is run by Bord Bia, Teagasc and Enterprise Ireland for new food start-ups (www.foodworksireland.ie). For more information on starting and marketing your food-based business, check www.bordbia.ie/industry/smallbusiness/.

If you need funding, try MicroFinance Ireland (www.microfinanceireland.ie) – and also the banks or credit unions. For a list of all the funding measures available in the Republic of Ireland, see https://supportingsmes.gov.ie.

You will need to write a business plan (including three years' financial projections) for many of the funding providers, while others have their own application forms. It's a good exercise to develop a business plan anyway as you'll get your ideas out of your head and onto paper. This will focus your mind and highlight any gaps in information you need to get. Some of the support agencies will help you put your business plan together.

There are also grants and finance schemes to help businesses implement environmental/green measures. For details, contact SEAI (www.seai.ie/business-and-public-sector/business-grants-and-supports), the Local Enterprise Offices' 'Green for Micro' programme, or in the UK the Business Climate Hub (www.businessclimatehub.uk).

My advice on funding: ask everyone! They will tell you quickly what is available and whether you're eligible. There are always new schemes, funding and training and mentoring programmes coming up. Don't assume anything – ask!

## Insurance

I strongly advise that you take out 'product liability' and 'public liability' insurance once you start selling your food. If you employ staff, then you'll need 'employer's liability' insurance too, and there may be other insurances to consider, including 'product recall' insurance. Product liability insurance provides cover for you if you become legally liable to a member of the public for bodily injury/ death/diseases and/or damages, expenses and costs as a result of a defective food product supplied by you or your company. Public liability insurance is important if members of the public have access onto your property. It provides cover for you if you become legally liable to a member of the public for bodily injury/death/diseases, damages, expenses and costs and/or damage to them or their property following an accident, in connection with your business. Get advice from an insurance broker.

In Ireland, try IOMST, the Irish Organisation for Market & Street Traders (www.iomst.ie) or MAST, the Markets Alive Support Team (www.mast.ie), for insurance for market traders. In the UK, try Mobilers Insurance Services (www.mobilers.co.uk) – or an insurance broker.

# 9

# TRAINING REQUIREMENTS

As a food producer, you (and your staff who are food handlers) are required by law to have completed food hygiene instruction/training. While strictly speaking, you don't actually have to complete a specific course, most Inspectors prefer it if you have done one, and my advice is to do a one- or two-day Food Hygiene or Food Safety training course. There are three categories of training;

- **Level 1:** The basic and minimum required by food handlers – they should have this within the first month of starting the job;
- **Level 2:** A step up – should be completed within 12 months maximum;
- **Level 3:** The training needed by supervisors and managers – should be as soon as possible.

In Ireland, food handlers must be supervised, and also instructed and/or trained in food hygiene based on the level of activity they are involved in. The free, on-line resource www.safefoodforbusiness.com (8 modules) covers FSAI Level 1 food safety.

In the UK (as per the FSA website), food handlers don't have to hold a food hygiene certificate to prepare or sell food. But food business operators must ensure that food handlers receive the appropriate supervision and training in food hygiene. This must be in-line with the area staff work in and to enable them to handle food safely.

A good starting point if you want to find a trainer is to look online, in your local paper or ask another producer for a referral. The Environmental Health Association of Ireland (www.ehai.ie) lists all the registered trainers in the Republic of Ireland and upcoming courses. Both the FSAI and FSA have information on their websites that outline the requirements for you and your staff in relation to training, so take a look there first.

Some sector-specific training courses and providers are mentioned in **Chapters 12** to **15**; other, more general courses and providers are listed below and in **Chapter 17**.

## Food Hygiene & Food Safety (HACCP)

Food safety training is essential in ensuring the preparation and service of safe food. You, or whoever is specifically involved in the design and implementation of the HACCP system, must understand the principles of HACCP – this means Level 3 training.

It is a legal requirement that anyone involved in making food, selling or distributing foods and working on food market stalls is adequately informed or trained. You and your helpers (whether paid or unpaid) must have a knowledge and understanding of food hygiene and be able to demonstrate good hygiene practices.

*Regulation EC 852/2004*, which covers the hygiene of foodstuffs, requires that food business operators (FBOs – that's you) must ensure:

- Food handlers are supervised and instructed and/or trained in food hygiene;
- Those responsible for the development and maintenance of HACCP have received adequate training in the application of the seven HACCP principles; and
- Everyone is trained in anything they're supposed to be trained in – ask your EHO/Inspector what applies to your business.

Sticking strictly to good hygiene principles is really critical when you are making your food products. You are legally obliged to ensure your food is safe for consumption. Food hygiene and food safety training is essential in ensuring the preparation and service of safe food.

Some providers of food hygiene and safety training are listed in **Chapter 17**.

Most primary food hygiene trainers also deliver HACCP training. If you prefer to do your training in your own time, then there are also many providers of food hygiene courses online.

After that, you can choose to do whatever training you like. Courses on everything from skills development (how to make cheese, etc.) to personal development to sales and marketing training are available around the country.

## Financial Management Training

When it comes to managing finances, it is a very good idea to do a short course, whether a one-day/evening course or as part of a Start Your Own Business course, to help you keep on top of things.

You must keep track of your costs, expenses and sales. If you find yourself working very hard, selling tons of product and yet are left with no money at the end of the year, then there is something wrong somewhere. Either you're undercharging, or your costs are too high, or both.

Sometimes, you can get free (or heavily subsidised) training through the Local Enterprise Offices or Rural Development Companies (LEADER).

## Other Training

The FSAI has some free online courses in Labelling, Microbiological Criteria, Food Contact Materials and more (www.fsai.ie/business-advice/running-afood-business/training-and-online-learning/elearning/). FSA and FSS have e-learning courses (www.food.gov.uk/businessguidance/online-food-safety-training/; www.foodstandards.gov.scot/business-and-industry/industry-specific-advice/manufacturers/).

I also advise you to do some training or at least read up on allergen management and acrylamide (for fried/roasted foods like chips, crisps, roast potatoes, roasted root vegetables, bread, coffee, biscuits and crackers, and baby food).

You also might consider taking a course in:

- Packaging technology;
- Product labelling and legislation;

- Product development, creativity and innovation;
- Sector skills – baking, sausage- and cheese-making, jam-making, yogurt and ice cream courses;

In terms of other short training courses, ask your LEO or Council for information about courses for small businesses generally – for example:

- Sales and marketing;
- Financial management for the small producer/business;
- Social media skills training (Facebook for Business, Instagram, TikTok, etc.);
- Chat GPT/AI;
- IT skills development;
- Personal development/confidence-building.

## Funding for Training

In Ireland, training through your LEO might be free or heavily subsidised. Subsidised training is also offered through the Skillnet Ireland network, so be sure to check (www.skillnetireland.ie).

In the UK, funding for training will vary by Council, so just make enquiries locally.

# 10
# BREAD & BAKING

## The Opportunity

Many people I talk to who are considering starting up a food business at home are thinking about baking bread – usually brown soda bread. If not bread, then celebration cakes, or cupcakes. There are not as many apple-tart bakers, for some reason.

While bread is an easy food to produce at home, you must first ask yourself: is there really an opening for yet another bread baker? What could you bake that's a little different? Perhaps you should consider using spelt flour or rice flour, adding seeds or going after the health food or 'free from ...' market, or trying sourdough.

A great selling point can be to tell your prospective customers what your food does not contain! You might think people would know that traditional brown or white soda bread does not contain yeast. But why make assumptions? It's always good to point these things out to shoppers; it will catch their eye that way (a flashy sticker can be good here) and help you make sales.

So, try to do something a little different from the usual. Check out what's not available, and try to fill a gap.

Most bread, cakes and fruit pies will sell all year round, even if only at weekends. There also will be increased demand around traditional family events – these offer big business opportunities for the local dessert-maker or caterer, especially now when the trend is to entertain the family at home rather than in a hotel or restaurant. You could put up a notice in your local shop or local community social media page.

There are broadly three main categories of breads, depending on the raising agent you use: soda bread (traditional Irish), yeast bread and sourdough bread.

Home-producers of yeast bread or sourdough will be competing with the large producers of sliced pans. You can't complete on volume or price, but you can complete on quality, flavour, style and craft.

# Ingredients & Production Requirements

The basic ingredients for yeast bread are simple: flour, water, yeast and salt. For soda bread, there is no absolute list, and you can add almost anything to it to make it different – seeds, sugar or treacle, raisins, you name it. Push sprigs of rosemary into focaccia bread before baking, or chop up fresh rosemary and add it with freshly ground black pepper to plain white soda bread, or add cheese and onions or sundried tomatoes to scone mix. Get as fancy as you like or keep it simple. The possibilities are endless.

### What you need

You need:

- Suitable, approved premises;
- A bowl for mixing – plastic, ceramic, whatever you like;
- A clean, smooth surface for rolling-out and cutting;
- An oven;
- A place you can leave the bread to cool;
- Space to store the baked loaves

You could decide to buy a bread-maker – a machine that takes a lot of the chore out of the process or you might prefer to stick with the fully hand-made method, elbow grease and all.

For packaging, you'll need tins, boxes, paper bags, plastic bags, foil trays, foil/paper inserts and trays for transporting the finished breads.

### Set-up costs

Set-up costs include the price of the equipment, although your own domestic oven, bowls and tins may suffice to begin with, albeit only allowing small quantities.

## Running costs

The main running costs involved are the ingredients, electricity/gas and labour. Unless you plan to wrap the bread, you won't need any packaging or labels, although you will need some sort of trays or baskets for carrying/transporting the loaves. As with everything else we have talked about, don't forget to include your own time into any cost calculations. The cost of marketing and distribution is also extra.

## Return on investment

The price at which you can sell your bread/buns/scones/cakes will probably be higher than commercially-produced varieties – consumers expect to pay more for hand-made, home-produced baked goods, provided the quality and taste are there.

Check local shops and see what other similar goods are being sold for. Maybe you'll only sell cupcakes or desserts at weekends.

Most shops will have a sale or return policy for baked goods, so you will have to take home what doesn't sell ('returns') at your own cost. Go easy initially with the volumes!

Keep an eye out for which varieties sell and which don't – and don't forget that there will be seasonal demand too.

# Sourdough Bread

While variations of sourdough bread can be found all over the world, and there is evidence that the ancient Egyptians made sourdough bread, it was during the California Gold Rush that the San Francisco Sourdough was born in the modern age, and sourdough has become synonymous with that city.

So what is sourdough bread anyway, how is it made? And how does it differ from other bread? The four main ingredients that go into making your loaf of bread are flour, water, yeast and salt. In fermentation, the job of the yeast is to produce carbon dioxide from the flour, which enables the dough to rise. Sourdough bread is made differently, it is naturally leavened in that there is no yeast added. Instead, it uses a 'starter', a fermented flour and water mixture that contains wild yeast and bacteria. This produces the unique tangy flavour and slightly chewy texture typical of sourdough.

To make a sourdough starter, flour and water are mixed together and left to ferment at room temperature. Yeast and bacteria (mostly *Lactobacillus sp.*) in the air ferment the sugars in the flour and produce gas. You will see the starter begin to bubble up after a couple of days as the gas is produced. Some people allow the fermentation process to run for anything from eight to 24 hours or even longer. The starter has to be fed more flour and water to stay alive (if you don't, you'll know all about it as it will start to smell really badly, and the starter will die). A starter is a living thing really, and some people even name their sourdough starter!

Interestingly, there is no EU definition of or legislation about what is meant by the term 'sourdough' or 'sourdough bread', although some countries such as Germany, France and Australia have their own national guidelines. In 2019, the FSAI's Artisan Forum, which is made up of food producers and industry experts, attempted to come up with an agreed definition of what can be called sourdough bread and the method by which it is made. For example, consideration was given to the list of permitted ingredients, the minimum fermentation time, etc. However, no agreement was reached, so a definition of sourdough bread has not yet been established.

Some people ask if sourdough bread is gluten-free and the answer is an emphatic No! Sourdough bread is made with wheat or rye flour usually, and these contain gluten. There is a lot of talk about whether sourdough bread can make unique health claims but there are in fact no approved health claims for sourdough bread in the EU.

## Gluten-free

'Gluten-free' products have experienced continued growth in demand. While it is estimated that only 1% to 2% of people in either Ireland or the UK have been properly diagnosed with coeliac disease, there are probably many others who have not yet been diagnosed, and another approximately 10% of the population who are gluten-intolerant. Other people don't eat wheat for whatever reason, by choice.

Coeliac disease is not a food allergy or intolerance, however, it is an autoimmune disease. It is a serious illness, where the body's immune system attacks itself when gluten is eaten. This causes damage to the lining of the gut and means that the body cannot properly absorb nutrients from food. So not a choice, and not to be taken lightly.

In the past, good quality gluten-free bread was hard to come by. In recent years, thankfully, improvements in baking techniques and the availability of gluten-free and other types of flour (rice, potato, etc.) and other ingredients have meant that good quality gluten-free breads are more readily available.

While most people do not have coeliac disease and choose gluten-free for personal reasons, you should still work to a high standard so that if you say 'gluten-free' on the pack then it is definitely gluten-free in the pack for this group of consumers. For the labelling requirements for proper 'gluten-free' food suitable for coeliacs, see **Chapter 7**.

Contamination during the baking process is a major hazard in a kitchen since your 'gluten-free' food can easily be contaminated with gluten from your other foods. Control here is critical and you really must get advice from your EHO or Inspector and from the Coeliac Society (www.coeliac.ie or www.coeliac.org.uk) about your set-up. The Coeliac Society's Food List team works with producers to make sure they comply with the standards for gluten-free foods and that no cross-contamination occurs during the manufacturing process.

To be absolutely sure that there is no cross-contamination, you will need a separate kitchen for your gluten-free products aimed at the coeliac market; this usually means a separate building. You need:

- Dedicated equipment and utensils;
- Very high standards for cleaning;
- A very well-organised kitchen or bakery.

So how do you manage to control this? Why, through your HACCP system, of course! (see **Chapter 3**).

In order for products to be gluten-free when they reach the consumer, you have to be absolutely sure that your baking process is tightly managed to prevent any contamination with gluten. Cross-contamination is the process by which a gluten-free product loses that status because it comes into contact with something that is not gluten-free.

Unless you are specifically aiming your foods at people with coeliac disease, when absolute certainty is paramount with regards to preventing cross-contamination, then one way to manage this is to make gluten-free products at the start of the production day when contamination from dust is at a minimum and all equipment and clothing are thoroughly clean. Then follow gluten-free products with gluten-containing products before cleaning. Alternatively, you could make your gluten-containing products on separate days from your gluten-free products, with a thorough cleaning in between.

FSAI has a very detailed guidance note on its website (www.fsai.ie) about producing foods that are gluten-free.

## Current Trends & Future Developments

Spelt flour, rice flour, sour dough, rye ... never has there been such a variety of baked goods on the market. The influence of eastern European cultures is very evident in the baked goods market, with many Polish bakeries operating across the country and selling in the main supermarket retailers. While some foods will always be a regular part of the grocery basket, and others including sourdough have become mainstream, pastries and cakes for example are considered as treats and luxuries and so will be purchased less often. Your bread and cakes will compete for sales against all varieties of baked goods, so keep an eye out for what the consumers are looking for. The health food market is a big one and always looking for new products.

## Case Study: Rustic Boowa

At the start of this book I mentioned how food is influenced by travel abroad, by immigrants arriving and introducing us to their food culture, by making foods that you want to eat but that you cannot buy locally. One great example of this is Rustic Boowa (instagram.com/rustic_boowa) in Co. Kerry, which was started by two Polish sisters, Zaneta Labuz-Czerwień and Ilona Koscielniak and their husbands Piotr (who is the main baker) and Pawel, during Covid. It started with home baking being sold from a table and gazebo, moving to a food truck at

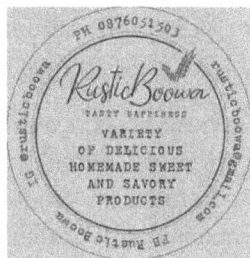

Banna Strand, and finally into a bricks and mortar bakery and café in Tralee.

A multi-award winning family business, their ethos is to use only organic flour and fresh, natural ingredients to make a delicious variety of sweet and savoury vegetarian and dairy-free (vegan) products. Only best quality ingredients are used, many from local farmers. Everything is made on the premises by hand every day, including a 48-hour sourdough. Zaneta emphasises the importance of returning customers who enjoy the quality of the foods and whose regular custom supports the business. With a commitment to sustainability, they also provide customers with the option to purchase a Too Good To Go bag of goodies at the end of the day (www.toogoodtogo.com/en-ie).

Growth plans include more B2B customers and they have recently opened another café in Ardfert. Some of their awards include *Blas na hÉireann* Gold in 2023 for their long proving bread and Best in Kerry and *Blas na hÉireann* Gold in 2022 for their signature Sweet Boowa.

# 11

# JAMS, PRESERVES & HONEY

## Jams & Preserves

Another very popular food made at home for sale locally are jams and preserves. In recent years, many home-producers have been foraging in the hedgerows and gardens and started making jam, apple jelly, lemon curd, fruit coulis, quince cheese (a sliceable, jelly-like preserve) and chutney. All of these are relatively low-risk from a food safety and hygiene point of view, and fairly easy to make in your home kitchen.

People love home-made jam and your local shop or Farmers' market is a good outlet, especially since many of these products have a long shelf life. So, if you have fruit trees, bushes, or canes, a glut of rhubarb, or access to fresh fruit or vegetables (whether from your own garden or a local grower), then this could be the start you are looking for.

One word of caution though: because it is relatively easy to make these products in your kitchen and because they are relatively low-risk, then the likelihood is that everyone else will be doing it too, which will mean more competition for you. So, do something different – even just slightly different.

### The opportunity

There are very many jam producers in the country: some large scale, some small. Don't let this put you off. If you have a good product and have no local competition from other home-based producers, then consumers will be happy to try your jam. What will make them buy it again? The usual: quality, taste and flavour. So, spend time developing your recipes.

If you can come up with a good recipe for strawberry jam, which is notoriously difficult to make as it doesn't set easily (since it contains low levels of pectin), then you could be on to a winner! Jams made with no added sugar (using fruit juice instead usually) are also very popular (albeit not low in sugar, so don't make any claims to this effect). The higher the fruit content in your jam, generally the better it will be.

## Ingredients & Production Requirements

The basic ingredients required for making jam, jelly or marmalade are fruit, sugar, acid, pectin and water. As with all food products, the fresher the ingredients, the better the product. Use only the best quality fruit, ensure it is just ripe and not bruised or damaged.

The acid and pectin content of fruit is important to consider, as these are required in order to achieve a good 'set' in the jam when the mixture cools down. All fruits contain pectin, but some have higher quantities than others. Apples, gooseberries, blackcurrants and redcurrants are all rich in pectin, whereas strawberries, cherries and pears contain very low levels of pectin. Blackberries, plums and raspberries contain medium amounts of pectin. For fruits with low/medium amounts of pectin, you may need to add commercial pectin to the recipe in order to ensure a good set. This is added when the fruit has been cooked and the flesh and skin have softened.

To test for pectin content, take one teaspoon of the juice from the cooked fruit, place it into a clear glass and allow it to cool for a couple of minutes. Then add three teaspoons of methylated spirits (which you can buy in a pharmacy or DIY shop). If a large firm clot forms, this indicates that the pectin levels are high and there is no need to add extra pectin. If you get a number of broken clumps, this indicates that there is insufficient pectin to get a good set, so a little commercial pectin should be added.

Follow the suppliers' instructions when using commercial pectin, as often the boiling time will be shorter after sugar has been added. The acidity of the fruit pulp also will influence the set, and as with pectin, fruits also differ in their acidity. Citrus fruits are acidic, while many other fruits such as blackberries, plums and raspberries have medium acidity, and strawberries and cherries are not at all acidic. When making jams with medium/low acid fruit, add one or two tablespoons of fresh lemon juice per kg of fruit at the beginning of cooking.

Commercial jams often contain less than 50g fruit per 100g. Homebased jam-makers should be aiming for 60g fruit/100g jam or higher, ideally. The legal minimum requirement is 35g/100g generally, although blackcurrants and quinces can be 25g/100g and there are some other exceptions. 'Extra jam' contains higher levels of fruit than the usual version. The additional fruit can be added in purée form.

Sometimes you will see labels on jam listing 'jam sugar' as an ingredient. This is sugar with pectin mixed into it (as it's a compound ingredient, the pectin should be listed separately – see **Chapter 7** for ingredients labelling requirements). Jam sugar often contains citric acid also, which acts as a preservative.

The FSAI guide (below) lists the permitted ingredients in jam according to EU law. Some of these are very specific, depending on the type of jam you are making. For example, red fruit juices can be used only in jam manufactured from rosehips, strawberries, raspberries, gooseberries, redcurrants, plums and rhubarb. Check the guide if you're not sure.

The legislation that tells you all this comes from EU *Directive 2001/116/EC*. The FSAI has a great guide called *Labelling of Jams, Jellies & Marmalade* on its website (www.fsai.ie) and the Food Standards Agency (www.food.gov.uk) also has a specific Guidance Note called *Jams & Similar Products*, with slight differences for Wales and Northern Ireland. Teagasc has produced a fact sheet, *Small Scale Production of Fruit Preserves*, which you can find on www.teagasc.ie.

## What you need

You need:

- Suitable, approved premises;
- A clean pot or vessel for boiling and simmering the fruit – don't use copper or unsealed cast iron pans as the natural acids in fruit will damage the surfaces of these pans, spoiling your jam or preserve;
- A method for sterilising the clean jars;
- An area where you can pour the hot jam into jars;

- A labelling area where the labels are applied to the jars after the lids are on;
- Space to store the packaged product.

## Set-up costs

Set-up costs include the price of the equipment, although your own pots and pans may suffice to begin with.

You will need space – although you might be surprised at first at how few jars you seem to get from a large amount of fruit and sugar and all your hard work!

## Running costs

The main running costs involved are ingredients (fruit, sugar, pectin, fruit juice if you are using it), packaging, electricity and labour. It is important that you include your own time into any cost calculations. Labour input can be high! The cost of marketing and distribution is extra.

You also will have to buy jars, lids, and labels. You must buy new jam jars every time. Legally, you are not allowed to re-use old jars from your cupboard (or anyone else's cupboard!) for your jam enterprise.

## Sterilising jars

There are a number of different ways that you can sterilise jars: oven, microwave or dishwasher. Ask your EHO or Inspector which one they would prefer you to use. The key thing to check, however, is that the jar must be absolutely clean first.

## Return on investment

The price you can sell your jam for will be higher than commercially-produced jam – consumers expect it to be more expensive. Check local shops and see what other home-made jam is being sold for. Around €2.99 or higher is not uncommon, even up to €5/£5 in Farmers' markets, and you need to allow for the retailer's margin too if selling through shops.

## How to make jams & preserves

Every jam-maker claims that they have a special skill when it comes to their own recipes, and perhaps they do!

It's best to make jam in relatively small quantities to give you better colour, flavour and clarity. The method is more or less as follows:

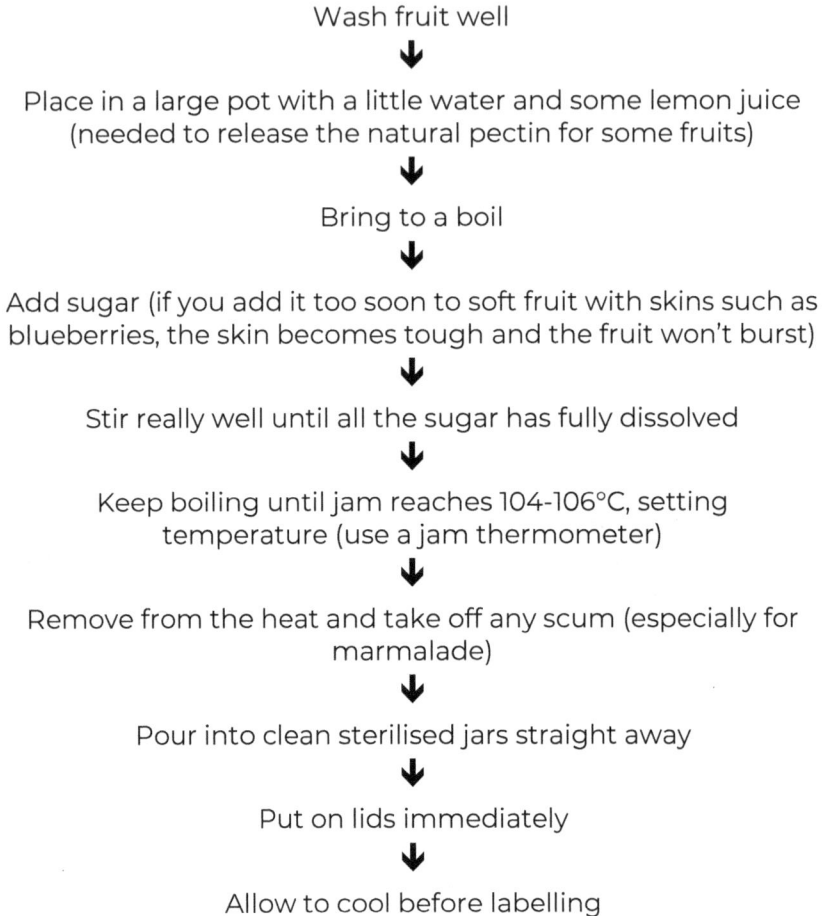

Wash fruit well
↓
Place in a large pot with a little water and some lemon juice (needed to release the natural pectin for some fruits)
↓
Bring to a boil
↓
Add sugar (if you add it too soon to soft fruit with skins such as blueberries, the skin becomes tough and the fruit won't burst)
↓
Stir really well until all the sugar has fully dissolved
↓
Keep boiling until jam reaches 104-106°C, setting temperature (use a jam thermometer)
↓
Remove from the heat and take off any scum (especially for marmalade)
↓
Pour into clean sterilised jars straight away
↓
Put on lids immediately
↓
Allow to cool before labelling

To test jam to see whether it is cooked enough and will set, you can:

- Dip a wooden spoon into the jam, holding the bowl of the spoon facing you. If the jam is ready, then two or three large drops will roll along the edge of the spoon forming almost a triangle of thick jam;
- Drop a teaspoon of jam onto a chilled saucer (chill the saucer in the freezer or fridge first); the jam should cool quickly to room temperature and thicken up;

- Put a spoonful of jam onto a plate, push the jam with your finger and if the skin wrinkles, then the jam is ready.

Otherwise, boil it up again.

## Current trends & future developments

Quince cheese, port-flavoured cranberry sauce, mixed fruit jams, jellies and various savoury chutneys are always popular. Consumers expect a choice, so if you want to differentiate yourself from the herd, then produce high-quality, good-flavour, seasonal varieties. Recently I've seen Strawberry with Champagne, Passionfruit, Rhubarb & Ginger, Blood Orange marmalade, Spiced Apple jelly, Sonata Strawberry jam, Fig jam, so possibilities are extensive!

## Specific labelling issues

The usual labelling information is mandatory, as already described in **Chapter 7**. In particular, note the following:

- The name under which the product is sold: For example, 'Raspberry Jam';
- Instructions for use, where necessary: For example, 'Reduced sugar jams must be kept in the fridge'.

The following labelling information is also mandatory under the specific labelling rules:

- **An indication of the fruit used in descending order:** For example, for rhubarb and ginger jam;
  o *The fruit content:* By including the words 'prepared with Xg of fruit per 100g';
  o *The total sugar content:* By the words 'total sugar content Xg per 100g'.

Where the residual content of sulphur dioxide exceeds 10mg/kg, you must indicate its presence on the list of ingredients – though most home-producers won't need to worry about this at all.

Very important! The name of the product, the fruit content and the total sugar content must appear in the same visual fields and in clearly visible characters.

## Case Study: Moran's Megajam

Kieron and Claire Moran trained in Dublin and worked for years in some of the country's best hotels and catering establishments. In the background, Kieron was perfecting his recipes for a range of jams and relishes. They set up their business in 2010 in Ballinagh, Co. Cavan, specialising in quality homemade jams, chutneys, relishes and pesto using fresh, locally-sourced ingredients, handmade to the same perfected recipes.

Kieron and Claire both understand the importance of product development and having a USP, so they came up with unusual and quirky recipes, including Peach & Bourbon, Pineapple & Malibu, Pear, Blackberry & Amaretto, Raspberry & Tiramisu, as well as all the usual flavours you would expect in jam. They also make marmalade and a No-Added Sugar range.

Moran's Megajam (www.moransmegajam.ie) has won many awards, including Silver at *Blas na hÉireann* – in 2019 for their Beetroot Relish and again in 2023 for their Tomato & Caramelised Red Onion Chutney. The range is sold through local artisan shops, craft butchers and SuperValu stores nationwide.

Sustainability is important, and Kieron and Claire are Gold members of the Bord Bia Origin Green Sustainability programme (www.origingreen.ie). When you buy online, the jars come protected in inflated cellulose packaging!

Moran's use social media really well, posting videos of jam being stirred or being poured into jars (you can almost smell the flavours!), or collaborating with @ChefShaneSmith, which is really good for engaging their customers. "We have a brand new website and online sales have never been busier thankfully", says Kieron.

## Honey

You may not remember the great Irish honey scandal of 2006! It was found that, of a number of producers surveyed, some were mislabelling their honey, claiming it was Irish when it was not. Local honey is always popular among shoppers, though the recent poor summers have reduced the volume of honey available. So, if you do produce Irish honey, then shout about it! There is a very useful factsheet on Honey Production on www.teagasc.ie.

If you keep bees and produce honey for sale, then you must register as a 'primary producer'. You can get the form from your local DAFM office or download it from www.agriculture.gov.ie (search for 'Registration as a Primary Producer of Honey') or in the UK contact the Food Standards Agency (www.food.gov.uk).

There are very specific rules relating to the labelling of honey. Products can only be marketed as 'honey' if they comply with the definition and compositional requirements as set out in *Directive 2001/110/EC* relating to honey. In the UK, the *Honey (England) Regulations 2015* apply. So it is best to familiarise yourself with them before labelling your jars.

Some of the most common types of honey are:

- **According to origin:** Such as blossom honey or nectar honey (honey obtained from the nectar of plants);
- **According to mode of production and/or presentation:** Such as chunk honey or cut comb in honey (honey that contains one or more pieces of comb honey).

The country or countries of origin where the honey has been harvested must be indicated on the label. If the honey originates in more than one EU Member State or third country, then the indication may be replaced by one of the following as appropriate (the EU law still applies in the UK until it gets updated) :

- 'Blend of EU honeys';
- 'Blend of non-EU honeys'; or
- 'Blend of EU and non-EU honeys'.

## Case Study: Olly's Farm Honey

In 2012, Olly Nolan set up a smallholding on a small piece of land in the Dublin mountains in the valley of Glenasmole, with the aim of becoming self-sufficient in relation to food combined with modern living. Olly now grows and produces far more than he can use and so he sells it to people who are interested in eating great natural food reared and grown organically on the farm. The range includes several different types of raw honey, as well as beef, pork and eggs.

**OLLY'S FARM**

**DUBLIN HONEY**

Olly's Farm (www.ollysfarm.ie) produces 100% raw, local, Irish honey (no blends!) that is available at different times throughout the year. And because of the true seasonal nature of the honey some of the products, such as the pressed heather honey, are in limited supply. All the honey comes from apiaries around South Dublin and North Wicklow. It is sold as raw honey; this means that the honey has minimal processing and is not pasteurised in any way.

Olly is a passionate bee farmer, who cares about his incredible honey bees who work hard. When he moved up to the smallholding, he had only started beekeeping about a month before and planned on keeping only a couple of colonies to supply honey for themselves. He now has over 300 colonies and counting!

You can buy Olly's multi-award winning honey, along with pollen and beeswax, from his website and in Supervalu and several independent shops around Dublin and Wicklow. Olly's Honey is now also available in the Avoca shops (www.avoca.com) and he is a Guaranteed Irish (www.guaranteedirish.ie) member.

Olly also runs farm tours all year round, showing how he runs his smallholding and honey farm. He also runs beekeeping experiences throughout the summer months where people get to learn everything about bees and honey, get in a bee suit and handle the bees – tasting lots of different types of honey from the many different apiaries where he keeps his bees.

# 12

# PLANT-BASED FOOD

Vegetarianism has been around for literally thousands of years, with evidence as far back as the 1st century. People choose not to eat meat for a variety of reasons – ethical, ascetic or environmental.

Vegetarians who eat no animal produced foods at all (like milk, eggs or honey) are vegans. It is estimated that 10% of the population in Ireland and the UK is either vegan (approx. 3%) or vegetarian (about 7%). Alongside that are the flexitarians, people who might eat vegan or vegetarian a couple of days a week or so.

With a rise in consumer awareness about the potential environmental impact of producing beef, for example, and the concerns around health, many consumers are choosing to reduce their meat intake. This offers an opportunity for food producers to develop a whole new range of foods, and what is definitely true is that there has been a huge increase in the variety and number of plant-based foods available on the market.

Growth in the global plant-based market is expected to exceed $480 billion by 2024 (according to BIS Research (www.bisresearch.com) in 2020).

## Terminology Explained

**Vegan products** do not contain any animal-based ingredients, such as meat, fish, dairy, eggs or honey. The production process must not use animal-derived products either, such as gelatine for clarifying juice or wine, or for strict vegans, even animal-based glue for product packaging.

**Vegetarian** foods exclude meat and fish, but may include ingredients such as some dairy, eggs, and honey.

For food, the term **plant-based** refers only to a processed product's ingredients. Plant-based foods do not contain any animal-sourced ingredients. Plant foods refer to unprocessed plants that are part of the human diet, such as fruit, vegetables, legumes and spices.

## Legislation & Food Safety

You cannot assume that simply because the food is meat/dairy-free, that it is low risk from a food safety point of view. Not at all. In fact, it is more likely that there may be a lot of handling and use of many ingredients in producing the food, so it is in fact more likely to be high risk and you will need to take all necessary precautions.

The same legislation that applies generally to small food producers in the EU applies here too: *Regulations EC 178/2002* (which sets out the general requirements of food law and food safety), *EC 852/2004* (the Hygiene of Foodstuffs) and the current equivalent in the UK (see **Chapter 16**).

## Developments

Years ago, the options for vegan ingredients were pretty limited. You had fruit and vegetables, of course, pulses and legumes, nut and seeds, but that was really it. However, with the development of this category, many ingredients which may have previously been virtually unknown are now more commonplace in usage among vegan food producers. Some examples of these include:

- **Soy:** Made from the soya bean, it can be used either unfermented (tofu, soy silk, edamame) or fermented (miso, tempeh, soy sauce);
  - o Tempeh is a source of protein;
  - o Soy is an allergen;
  - o Textured Vegetable protein (TVP) is made from soybeans;
- **Seitan:** Made from wheat gluten (an allergen) and water. It is a key ingredient in many plant-based foods as a substitute for meat. It's high in protein and minerals and low in carbohydrate;

- **Teff:** A cereal grass, high in iron, is gluten-free and grows mainly in East Africa. It is ground into flour and used to make flatbread;

- **Chia seeds:** Good as a source of omega-3 fatty acids, but there are legal limits as to how much you can add to some foods, due to their impact on digestion. The addition of Chia seeds in breakfast products is limited to <10% under EU legislation (*EU 2017/2470*), thereby restricting the levels at which it could be added as well as potential benefits;

- **Yeast flakes or nutritional yeast:** Basically deactivated brewer's yeast. It may be fortified (with vitamins and minerals) or unfortified. It is commonly used in vegetarian and vegan cooking to provide a rare non-animal form of vitamin B12. It has a distinctive umami and is often used to provide a cheesy flavour;

- **Soy, oat almond and other alternatives to milk:** According to both EU and GB law, the term 'milk' can only refer to milk from animal origin. Years ago, you might have seen labels saying Oat Milk, or even Oat 'Mylk', but that is not allowed, and now you'll notice Oat Drink, Almond Drink, etc.

## Case Study: Thanks Plants

Aisling Cullen is no stranger to the food industry, having previously run a coffee house and restaurant before moving into food production. She set up Thanks Plants in 2020, having moved back to Ireland in 2017. Aisling is passionate about plant-based cooking, and she wanted to come up with a product that was wholesome and flavourful. Since she started making her own meatless meals using whole food ingredients, Aisling has never looked back.

Her motivation is both for her love of animals and for the environment. "We can all do our bit to help these causes by reducing or eliminating meat from our diet with really simple changes to our favourite dishes", says Aisling.

Thanks Plants (www.thanksplants.co) won silver at the National Start-Up awards in 2022 and Best Green SME Food & Beverage

Producer of the Year in 2021 at the Green Food & Beverage Producer Awards.

You can buy the Thanks Plants range in supermarkets, including Tesco, Aldi, Fresh Supermarkets, and in many independent retailers, as well as foodservice through Musgrave Marketplace.

# 13

# CHEESE, ICE CREAM, YOGURT & BUTTER

While the majority of the dairy market is controlled by very large national and international producers, there are many artisan producers making high-quality dairy produce for sale all over the country. In this chapter, we look at how you might go about developing a range of dairy products such as farmhouse cheese, ice cream, yogurt, butter or raw milk products.

As with all new food brands, the main force driving the market for dairy products comes from consumer trends. Since the removal of the EU milk quota in 2015, non-farmers can purchase milk from farmers without restriction. However, the barriers to entry for dairy products are high in terms of costs and legislation. Registration and approval of premises making dairy produce falls under DAFM's remit in Ireland.

## Cheese

Farmhouse cheese-making virtually died out in Ireland until the late 1970s. For at least 25 years before then, cheese-making in Ireland had been confined almost exclusively to large-scale factory production, mainly concentrating on cheddar production and mainly owned by the big dairy co-ops. However, today Ireland ranks third in the world (behind Denmark and New Zealand) in terms of cheese production *per capita*. The production of quality Irish cheese has expanded greatly, including makers of cows, goats, sheep and even buffalo cheese.

Halloumi cheese also has become very popular. In 2021, it won a Protected Designation of Origin (PDO) status from the EU, meaning that only approved producers from Cyprus can market the cheese under that name.

The provenance of cheese is of particular importance when branding and marketing it. Cheeses are associated not only with where they are made but also often with the individual cheese-makers themselves. Traceability of farmhouse cheese can extend not just to a region or townland, but also often to a family.

## The opportunity

It is estimated that there are about 1,800 different varieties of cheese in the world. So you might well wonder if there is room for any more. As with all other foods, if your cheese has a unique, great flavour, is made locally or regionally and is of top quality, then cheese-lovers will buy it.

In Ireland, the majority of cheese producers in Ireland were traditionally located in the major dairy-producing counties in the south of the country where the land is better for dairy cows. Typical Irish cheeses include both hard and soft varieties, but there are also lots of goats cheese, raw milk cheeses, sheep cheese and even buffalo mozzarella (the buffalo were imported!). You can find a great (albeit incomplete) list on www.bordbia.ie/farmhouse-cheese/.

In England, there are some fantastic unique regional cheeses – Cheddar, Red Leicester and Stilton, of course – and others with great names, including Cornish Yarg, Stinking Bishop and Ticklemore. In Scotland, you've got Minger, Tinto, Tito and Lanark Blue, with Caerphilly, Black Bomber and Perl Wen among a fantastic selection from Wales (www.visitwales.com/things-do/food-and-drink/cheese-experiences-wales/). You can probably guess that many names originate in the regional dialects and language.

## Market & distribution

The main market for artisan farmhouse cheese is domestic, although some producers are exporting. As with any new food, it is essential to carry out market research in advance to determine what gaps there may be in the market, whether local or national.

Almost all supermarkets now have artisan cheeses in their main fridges, as do many smaller and specialist shops. Sheridan's Cheesemongers (www.sheridanscheesemongers.com) in Meath and Horgan's in Cork (www.horgans.com) are among the largest countrywide distributors of specialist cheese. The Traditional Cheese Company (www.traditionalcheese.ie) supplies retail and wholesale brands, the majority of which are produced in Ireland.

In the UK, there are many distributors, including Neal's Yard Dairy (www.nealsyarddairy.co.uk), Grate (www.gratenewcastle.co.uk), or La Fromagerie (lafromagerie.co.uk), although a Google search will yield a long list you can start with. Many small producers reach the shelves through various retailers' food producer development programmes (see **Chapter 6**).

## Production

A useful *Farmhouse Cheese Factsheet* is available on www.teagasc.ie, which gives some facts and figures and describes the general production methods. Note that quark and soft cheeses are considerably easier to make compared to hard cheese varieties.

According to Eddie O'Neill, author of the Teagasc factsheet, what you need are:

- Suitable approved premises;
- A stainless steel vessel where milk can be converted into cheese;
- A moulding/pressing area where the curds are formed into their final shape;
- A brine tank (most cheeses) to salt the cheese;
- A ripening room where the cheese is held under the right conditions of temperature and humidity;
- A packaging area where the cheese is weighed and packed prior to distribution;
- A cold room or refrigerator to store the packaged product.

The FSAI and Teagasc have a handy workbook called *Food Safety Workbook for Farmhouse Cheesemakers*, which can be downloaded free (www.fsai.ie/publications/).

## How is cheese made?

Every cheese-maker has their own little secret about their recipe and what they do at each step to distinguish their cheese from all the others – but, in general, the more moisture there is in the cheese, the softer it will be. Soft cheese also tends to have less fat than hard cheese.

Some cheese must be kept to mature for a specified time, at a particular temperature and with certain other conditions to produce the quality and flavour desired. Some examples of mature cheese include Cheddar, Gruyère and Parmigiano Reggiano.

Here is a general overview of cheese-making:

Pour milk into a vat or container

↓

Add starter culture to ripen the milk

↓

Add rennet to produce curds and whey

↓

Separate the curds from the whey

↓

Press the curds into moulds

↓

Turn the moulds to form the shape and release more whey

↓

Apply pressure if a hard cheese is being made

↓

Add salt, if required

↓

Leave it to ripen (if desired)

↓

Pack and label

↓

Off to the shops!

## Set-up costs

Set-up costs include the price of the equipment, premises and/or conversion of existing buildings. You may have an existing building on your property, such as your garage or an old barn or outhouse, that could be converted into cheese-making units. It is extremely difficult to give indicative figures for costs where the conversion of existing buildings is required, as the work required will vary from one premises to another, depending on its state of repair. Whether a new premises or conversion, the costs of ensuring that the buildings meet hygiene regulations could be high. Advice on conversion requirements can be given on an individual basis by your Department advisor or Inspector.

The range of equipment needed can cost anything between €10,000 and €30,000. Some equipment suppliers are listed in **Chapter 17**.

## Running costs

The main direct costs involved are milk, ingredients, electricity, packaging and labour. It takes about 10 litres of milk to make 1kg of cheddar cheese. Rennet costs about €6 for 50ml. It is important that producers cost their own time into any business plan/cost calculations, as the labour input can be high.

The cost of marketing and distribution is extra, and distribution costs in particular can affect the overall viability of the business.

## Return on investment

The price you can sell your cheese for will vary depending on whether it is a speciality cheese and how far you are away from your market (as distribution costs will impact on your price). The period from production to time of sale could be up to six months, so being realistic, it is highly likely that cheese producers will have a negative cash flow in their first year.

## Current trends & future developments

Artisan cheeses have an international reputation for flavour and quality. Goats cheese is now commonplace and sheep and buffalo cheese are growing in popularity.

There are a few cheese-makers who use raw milk in the production of their cheeses. Caution is key when it comes to working with raw milk, and it is best to follow advice. A very high level of hygiene management is critical to ensure food safety when using raw milk, as it may contain disease-causing bacteria if not handled properly. The FSAI has issued a leaflet, *Health Risks from Unpasteurised Milk*, which is available to download on www.fsai.ie. The regulations on using and selling raw milk and raw milk products vary between Scotland (where it is banned), Northern Ireland, England and Wales. Check out www.food.gov.uk for information.

You will find some useful information from members of Cáis, the Association of Irish Farmhouse Cheese-makers (www.irishcheese.ie).

## Case Study: Rockfield Dairy

Rockfield Dairy is owned and run by Michael and Aisling Flanagan and is a sheep dairy business based in Co. Mayo, producing milk, yogurt and cheese made from sheep milk under the brands Velvet Cloud (www.velvetcloud.ie) and Rockfield Semi-hard Irish Farmhouse Cheese, as well as Cloonbook semi-hard Irish Farmhouse cheese.

"Sheep milk has a higher nutritional value than cows or goats milk, and suits people who may be intolerant to cows milk. It has a naturally sweeter creamier taste", says Aisling.

Out of thousands of cheeses, in 2019 Rockfield Cheese was awarded a Silver at the World Cheese Awards. In 2022, Rockfield Sheep's cheese won Best Artisan Cheese in Ireland and Best Sheep Cheese in the UK and Ireland at the Artisan Cheese Awards in the UK.

You can buy Rockfield Cheese and Velvet Cloud from their online shop, in speciality food stores, health food stores, speciality food stores nationwide and in large retailers, including selected Tesco, SuperValu and Dunnes Stores. All of their products are much sought after by chefs in high-end restaurants and hotels.

# Farmhouse or Home-made Ice Cream

Ice cream is made by freezing and aerating a mixture of ingredients, including dairy milk, sugar, flavours and water. The composition of ice cream varies, but is usually about 12% milk fat, 11% non-fat milk solids, 15% sugar and the rest of the ingredients plus water accounting for the balance. The Irish 1952 legislation says that ice cream must have a minimum of 10% sugar, but watch this space, that law is still under review.

For farmhouse, traditional or home-made ice cream producers, provenance again plays an important role in marketing the product, with the name of the farm, locality or producer often the main focus of the brand.

## History

It seems that everyone from the Chinese to the Italians and Americans lay claim to having invented ice cream!

In China, during the Tang period (AD 618-907), buffalo, cows and goats milk was heated and allowed to ferment. This 'yogurt' was then mixed with flour for thickening and camphor for flavour and was chilled before being served.

Italian gelato dates back to the 16th century. Most stories give the credit to Bernardo Buontalenti, a native of Florence, Italy, who delighted the court of Catherine de Medici with his creation. Italians almost certainly introduced gelato to the rest of Europe, with Sicilian-born Francesco Procopio dei Coltelli being one of the most influential individuals in the history of gelato – he was one of the first to sell it to the public.

In 1843, an American housewife Nancy Johnson invented the hand-cranked ice cream churn. She patented her invention and sold the patent for $200 to a Philadelphia kitchen wholesaler which, by 1847, had made enough freezers to satisfy the high demand. From 1847 to 1877, more than 70 improvements to ice cream churns were patented.

## The opportunity

The market for speciality ice creams continues to grow and there are many artisan and farmhouse producers in operation across Europe. The premium or luxury end of the market has grown too and it looks like this trend is set to continue. While consumers are increasingly concerned for their health, with lower fat ice cream made with natural ingredients without compromising on taste an emerging opportunity, indulgence in premium, luxury ice cream is always in demand.

In 2022, European consumers ate 3.2 billion litres of ice cream. That's right – 3.2 billion! Germany made the most, followed by France, then Italy. Ireland has the fifth highest consumption of ice cream *per capita* in Europe, with almost 11kg of ice-cream per person per year and a retail market value of approx. €150m. In the UK, nine out of 10 people buy ice cream, just under 6 litres each, but the market is worth £1.7bn or 365 million litres per year (according to 2022 figures)! The ice cream sector is always affected by any downturn in the economy, as are other luxury or 'special treat' foods. But, if staying in is the new going out, then good quality ice cream will always be in demand as an indulgence. Chocolate flavour is still a top seller but Cookies & Cream, Salted Caramel and Rum & Raisin are also very popular. Anyone who has visited an ice cream or gelato parlour on holiday will be very familiar with the huge range of flavours available.

Since I've mentioned it, what's the difference between ice cream and gelato? Well, ice cream contains more cream, so more butterfat than gelato. Ice cream also is churned more slowly than gelato, so tastes and feels creamier in your mouth.

Consumers usually assume luxury ice cream will be full of dairy cream, so it could be very worthwhile trying to develop reduced fat versions in your range. Interesting new flavours are a good way to get the consumer's attention – for example, Cinnamon & Cashew, Black Tea, Lemon Curd or Sweet Potato even! Gin & Tonic flavour is another one that caught my attention recently! There are also opportunities to target consumers who want flavours targeted at children.

*Note:* You cannot make ice cream allergen-free or vegan unless you remove the cows milk and eggs (if you're using eggs) – and then imminent EU legislation will mean you won't be able to call it ice cream any longer!

## Production method

You can buy ice cream machines ranging from 1 litre in size up to commercial scale, depending on how big a batch you want to make. You can start making it by hand and then move on to at least a partial batch manufacturing process. The recipe is a matter of trial and error.

To use fresh fruit or liquid flavours? To add egg or not? And you will have to play around with the best method to give you the flavour and consistency you want.

Teagasc's *Ice Cream Factsheet* (www.teagasc.ie) gives some facts and figures and describes the general commercial production method.

As for all food products, you will need premises that meet the EU hygiene legislation, and you must notify your local EHO or Inspector. For ice cream production, you need an approved processing area, a cold room and a freezer room, an area to store dry ingredients and an area to store packaging. Equipment for processing ranges in price enormously and can be quite expensive.

One method I came across a few years ago is making ice cream using liquid nitrogen. A little gimmicky perhaps, and a bit dangerous maybe, but it's certainly impressive. If you get a chance, visit Chin Chin Labs in Camden Market, London to try it yourself (www.chinchinlabs.com).

## Case Study: Scúp Gelato

Willie Devereux, the former Wexford hurler, set up Scúp (www.scupgelato.com) with his mother Siobhán in 2014. Since then, the family-run business has been producing and supplying Ireland's most luxurious gelato to the country's finest hotels and restaurants. Their aim is simple: make the best gelato using only the highest quality ingredients sourced locally and internationally, starting first with Ireland's amazing milk and cream.

From the beginning, Willie and Siobhán were clear that quality and authenticity were key to their USP. In the early days, when they were starting the business, the family hired a gelato master from Italy, bringing him to Wexford to show them how to create the product they wanted to sell.

Over the years, the relationships that they have developed with Ireland's top chefs has enabled the small team to craft the very best gelato. "With a blend of delicious flavours and keeping air quantity to

a minimum, it is sure to dazzle your taste buds with every spoonful", says Willie.

In 2022, having won several awards, they took the decision to expand into the retail market and Scúp is now available in shops and supermarkets. They do occasional pop-ups, including at Brown Thomas and Avoca, and are frequently found at food festivals and events.

# Farmhouse Yogurt

Yogurt has been a vital form of calcium in the diet in South Eastern Europe and Asia Minor for thousands of years. However, it was largely unknown outside these regions until scientific research suggested a direct link between yogurt and fermented milk and the unusually long lifespan enjoyed by Bulgarian people. Though this link was never proven, yogurt quickly gained popularity across Europe and the USA, particularly after fruit and sugar was added to improve the flavour and it began to be produced commercially.

Yogurt was introduced into the UK market in the 1960s and was seen as a health food, brought in from Switzerland. It came into the Irish dairy market in the 1970s and soon became a household essential, particularly popular with younger consumers.

## Market

Adults eat the most yogurt, accounting for about 75% of the total market. Family yogurts, especially those aimed at young families, followed by large pots, are most popular. Yogurt is eaten most often for breakfast and as a snack. Diet or low fat yogurts are beginning to lose popularity a bit as consumers become more aware of the ingredients they contain, especially sugar.

Indulgence is always attractive for consumers, so yogurts in glass containers or with specialised ingredients, like Madagascan Vanilla, or with authentic provenance will appeal. The health market continues to grow and yogurts with high protein have emerged. Other trends include sheep milk yogurt and fermented drinks such as kefir, both targeting the health market.

## Opportunity

While there are very many large commercial producers in the market, consumers are always interested in something new and locally-made, and are prepared to pay for it. Shoppers see yogurt as an everyday standard purchase but competition is fierce, it's a very crowded shelf. Any new producer should consider their target market, branding and USPs, particularly if they aim to compete with the big manufacturers.

## Production method (small batch)

Yogurt is produced by the bacterial fermentation of milk. The bacteria used to make yogurt are called 'yogurt culture'. Fermentation of the lactose in the milk by these bacteria produces lactic acid, which acts on the milk protein to give yogurt its texture and its characteristic flavour. So now you know!

There are two main types of yogurt: set and stirred. Set yogurt results when the incubation/fermentation of the milk takes place in the final container/packaging in which it is sold. Stirred yogurt, however, is produced after fermentation has been carried out in bulk, prior to final cooling and packaging.

You can make either plain or natural yogurt, fruit yogurt (by adding fruit and sweeteners) or flavoured yogurt (synthetic flavours and colours).

Frozen yogurt is made in the same way as the more common refrigerated kind, but it is then deep-frozen to -20°C (and it might need more sugar and stabiliser to withstand the freezer temperatures).

The yogurt culture is usually made up of *Lactobacillus* and *Streptococcus* bacteria. However, you don't have to start growing the bacteria yourself (!); you can buy it or use a commercially-produced yogurt as a convenient source of starter bacteria. Generally, a mixture of *Lactobacillus* and *Streptococcus* has been used to produce the yogurt and are still present in the starter.

The milk is first heated to 90°C to kill any undesirable bacteria and to denature the milk proteins so that they set together rather than form curds. The milk is then cooled to about 40°C to 43°C for incubation (or you can cool it completely and reheat it later). The bacteria culture is then added, and the temperature is maintained for four to seven hours to allow fermentation. If you are adding fruit or flavours, add them after fermentation. Altogether, preparation time for a small batch at home in your kitchen can take six to eight hours (or overnight). You can find recipes and procedures for making yogurt in recipe books and elsewhere. Of course, you can buy a yogurt-making machine too!

The ingredients for a typical 500g batch of plain yogurt are:

- 500ml whole pasteurised milk (cows, goats, sheep);
- 25g dried milk powder (optional);
- 3 tbsp (75g) live, plain whole-milk yogurt – starter culture.

The ingredients costs for this 500g batch are:

|  | € |
| --- | --- |
| Milk (a litre of milk costs around €0.30 if buying direct from farm or about €1.05 from a shop) | 0.15 / 0.55 |
| Good plain yogurt costs about €0.50/100g, 75g required as starter culture | €0.375 |
| **Total cost for ingredients per 500g batch** | **€0.525 / 0.925** |

# Butter & Other Dairy Products

As well as cheese, ice cream and yogurt, other dairy products have emerged over the past few years, including frozen yogurt, traditional country butter, butter flavoured with black pepper, garlic, sea salt, chilli, sun-dried tomato, herbs or 'Nduja sausage even, and brandy butter or brandy cream at Christmas.

## Registration

As for all food producers, dairy producers must be registered with DAFM (Ireland) or their local Council (UK).

In the Republic, anyone who wants to make a dairy product or process milk for direct human consumption must contact the Dairy Hygiene Division (057 869 4355/dairyhygiene@agriculture.gov.ie) within the Department of Agriculture (DAFM), which will provide further details on the registration/approval process, including application forms and an information pack. This pack includes copies of the relevant legislation and has a requirement for a TB Control Plan (for goats milk and other non-bovine milk producers), as well as information on all other aspects of milk and dairy production.

# Case Study: Abernethy Butter

Allison and Will Abernethy inherited their butter-making skills from previous family generations and, in 2005, decided to turn their hobby into a business.

Initially going to local agricultural and vintage shows to demonstrate how cream is churned and turned into butter, they soon realised there was a demand for their product.

The range of flavours includes salted and unsalted butter, dulse butter (made from a seaweed very closely associated with Northern Ireland), black garlic butter, chipotle chilli and smoked paprika, truffle, and Christmas butter. Such a great case study for product development and range extension!

Abernethy Butter is made with care and love. Top quality cream is sourced from a local dairy and there is a focus on quality and flavour above all else. The butters are slow churned in small batches, giving them their distinct colour and flavour. Time and effort is spent on the production process to ensure they maintain the quality they want.

Abernethy Butter (www.abernethybutter.com) can be found in many prestigious shops and restaurants across the UK.

In 2024, Allison and Will took the decision to retire, but happily the business has been taken on by Peter Hannan, an award-winning food producer in his own right (www.hannanmeats.com) and champion of Glenarm Shorthorn Beef.

## *Raw Milk*

Pasteurisation of milk destroys harmful bacteria but may also destroy nutrients present naturally in the milk. It has been claimed that raw milk may be beneficial for asthma sufferers. Restrictions on the sale of raw milk mean that, provided a raw milk producer is selling less than 30 litres per week within a 20 km radius, it can be sold directly to the consumer or through shops. If raw milk is used to make a raw cows milk product, the producer must inform their inspector as to where they are sourcing the milk, as herds providing raw milk for the production of raw milk product are subject to two TB tests annually.

For more information, contact Raw Milk Ireland (www.rawmilkireland.com) or the Raw Milk Producers Association (www.rawmilkproducers.co.uk) and the appropriate Department of Agriculture, as well as the FSAI, FSA or Food Standards Scotland.

### Goats milk products

Goats cheese is everywhere on menus. Apart from the great flavour of goats milk (though not for everybody!) and goats cheese, many people choose these foods because goats milk is often associated with some health benefits, particularly in the case of asthma and eczema. Application for registration and approval for production is made in the normal way through the Department of Agriculture.

## Conclusion

Anyone who is considering becoming a new entrant to cheese, yogurt or ice cream production is best advised to think carefully. Dairy production is not for the faint-hearted, not least because of the costs and legislation involved and the competition in the market.

# 14

# FLESH, FISH & FOWL

In this chapter, we look at how best to approach the development of a range of value-added raw meats, including sausages, pies and other foods. The information is relevant for farmers producing livestock, butchers, who may or may not have their own supply of meat, and other food producers who are neither farmers nor butchers.

The production of value-added meat products has evolved from kitchen to butcher to factory. However, the quality of the meat, the key ingredient, is important in terms of producing flavour and eating quality.

## Consumer Trends

There is no doubt that the majority of consumers still enjoy traditional style meals with meat at the centre. The importance of protein in the diet is very much in focus. The appeal of everyday products that serve up a touch of premium remains popular, as are oven-ready meat dishes. An opportunity presents itself for butchers and producers of meat-based foods to meet this demand.

Some butchers are now producing good quality value-added meat products like sausages, stir fries and casserole mixes, with other pig, beef and lamb farmers producing prepared joints, but perhaps not adding value beyond that due to lack of skills and/or facilities. We're talking more than Chicken Maryland or Chicken Kiev here, by the way! Salami, black and white puddings, beef jerky, cured meats, air dried meats, venison sausages, chicken breast stuffed with goats cheese and sun-dried tomato, wrapped in prosciutto – all have featured in small butcher shops over the past few years.

Irish grass-fed beef is recognised worldwide for its quality. In Ireland, the added-value meat market, including exports, is over €900m, and, in the UK, the added-value market is worth about the same. Trends in the sector include meatballs in sauce, stuffed joints with raw vegetables in a tray, straight-to-oven, smoked sausages and premium sausages (with at least 80% meat). There is always a demand from consumers for good quality, locally-produced, value-added meat products that provide a 'meal solution'.

Working in co-operation with other producers can be very useful – for example, the local butcher supplying meat to a local pasty-maker, who then sells their ready-to-cook pasties in the butcher's shop. Selling value-added foods through butcher shops that have supplied the meat is a really good way to co-operate, each promoting the other.

Breed branding is becoming a more common feature, with breeds such as Angus and Wagyu (Kobe) becoming better known, along with Dexter and Irish Moiled beef. Be sure to promote the quality of the meat from the breed, especially if it is niche or already has good brand recognition. Angus beef's association with quality is well-known and is positioned as a cut above 'ordinary' beef. Brands within retail and food service are increasingly playing on consumers' apparent growing appreciation of Angus beef.

The range of potential value-added products includes:

- Sausages;
- Steak burgers;
- Oven ready meals – stuffed joints, with or without vegetables;
- Stir fries with sauce and/or vegetables;
- Casserole mixes (with vegetables);
- Meatballs in tomato sauce;
- Pasties and pies.

In the case studies that follow, you will see some good examples of the high standards that can be achieved by small producers. Note how each has personalised their business and promotes tradition and provenance as a unique selling point (USP).

## Case Study: The Cornish Pasty

Did you know that at least 120 million Cornish pasties are made each year in the UK? So says the Cornish Pasty Association (www.cornishpastyassociation.co.uk), and they know a thing or two about it! A proper Cornish pasty contains at least 12.5% meat and a minimum of 25% vegetables (only potato, turnip or swede, and onion may be used). It also has both Geographical Origin (UK protected), and registered PGI in the EU (see **Chapter 6**).

Pasties have been mentioned in cookbooks for centuries, and in fact the name is thought to have originated from France, with old French recipes going back to the 13th century bearing strong similarities to the English variety. The pasty really came into its own in Cornwall though, where it was eaten by miners who could carry it in their pockets! It's a half-moon or D-shape pastry, folded over with the filling inside, and crimped to seal the edge. Then it is all baked in the oven.

As with all foods that travel as people move for work, the pasty evolved and, in England, you will also find the Bedfordshire Clanger and the Bacon Badger. Around the world, and in all cultures, many countries have their own versions: there's the *empanada* in South America, the *calzone* pizza, and the *sambousek* that is popular in the Middle East, as well as throughout Asia and Africa.

Maybe you can develop a local or regional pasty-style food using local ingredients!

## Production Requirements

Producing raw or cooked meat products in the kitchen at home isn't really feasible. Meat products are considered to be high-risk, so there is no avoiding a dedicated place in which to prepare your foods.

Unless you are already a butcher, you'll need access to or to partner with a butcher who can offer you good quality cutting and production facilities. You might not be able to afford to buy a sausage-making machine straight away, but perhaps your local friendly butcher would make the sausages or burgers for you, to your recipe, under contract.

If you are planning to make cooked meats, then you must have physically-separated raw and cooked areas. This is no small undertaking and should not be entered into lightly. It simply cannot be done at home.

For raw meat products, what you will need is a combination of some or all of the following:

- Suitable dedicated approved premises;
- Dedicated preparation area;
- Store for dry ingredients and for packaging;
- Sausage machine, mincing and mixing machines, knives, chopping boards and so on;
- A packaging area where the finished product is weighed and packed;
- A cold room to store the packaged product.

The capital costs of building and equipping a medium-sized facility (115m²/1,250sq.ft.) might be as much as €100,000 if you are starting from scratch, assuming you have a site already. Conversion of an existing garage or other premises may be cheaper, though it depends on the conversion work that needs to be done. Equipment costs vary and are available from the suppliers listed at the end of this chapter.

Nonetheless, the word on the street is that margins on sausages are very high, and that they are a valuable product for butchers – see more below.

## Case Study: Coopershill Venison

Coopershill in Co. Sligo has been in the O'Hara family since it was built in 1774, with the 8th generation now calling it home. Approximately 200 fallow deer roam the fields at Coopershill and are grass-fed throughout spring and summer. Mother and son, the inimitable Lindy and Simon, encourage farm visits so that consumers of Coopershill Venison can see first-hand the importance that they attach to the animals' welfare

(www.coopershill.com/venison.html). Coopershill is currently converting to Organic.

The advantage of farmed over wild venison is that they know the exact age of each animal and therefore can guarantee flavour and tenderness of the meat. High in iron and a range of vitamins, very lean and low in saturated fat, venison is the perfect red meat for anyone who cares about their cholesterol levels but still enjoys an exquisite meal.

You can buy Coopershill Venison by contacting them directly or ordering through their website.

## Case Study: Thornhill Duck

Surrounded by animals and fresh food all his life on the family's working farm, there was only ever one path Kenneth Moffitt could and wanted to take. When he was just 19, he started to rear a small number of free range geese on a specialised diet of natural feed for the Christmas and Easter markets. Locals quickly snapped up his produce, with word of mouth reaching hotels and restaurants in the region.

Spotting a niche for high quality poultry, he began to rear ducks. Twenty-three years later, Kenneth still operates from his farm in Blacklion, Co. Cavan, and supplies the many local hotels and restaurants in the region that first supported him.

Word-of-mouth has led to national demand and the award-winning Thornhill Duck (www.thornhillduck.com) now supplies some of Ireland's leading chefs, hotels and restaurants, including Neven Maguire's MacNean House & Restaurant.

## Sausages

It's hard to beat a good meaty sausage, with smooth mash, gravy and fried onions. Sausages have been around for about 5,000 years, with earliest mention of them coming from Mesopotamia in the Middle East. Sausage types include:

- **Raw** sausages that are usually made from pork, but also beef, lamb or chicken, which have to be cooked before eating; these include the

Bratwurst from Germany, and the English Cumberland (that's the curled up one) and Lincolnshire sausage varieties;

- **Cured** (like pepperoni or salami) or smoked sausage (such as the Polish Kielbasa) which is often, but not always, eaten cold.

- **Spreadable** sausage, like 'Nduja (which is delicious!) is more unusual, but chorizo is commonly used in homes in Ireland and the UK now; it may be smoked or unsmoked, but must be cooked before eating;

- **Blood** sausage or black pudding as it is called in Ireland.

So many varieties from the world over. But here we will focus on raw sausages, the ones we're most familiar with the Ireland and the UK.

## How to make sausages

The process of making sausages is as follows:

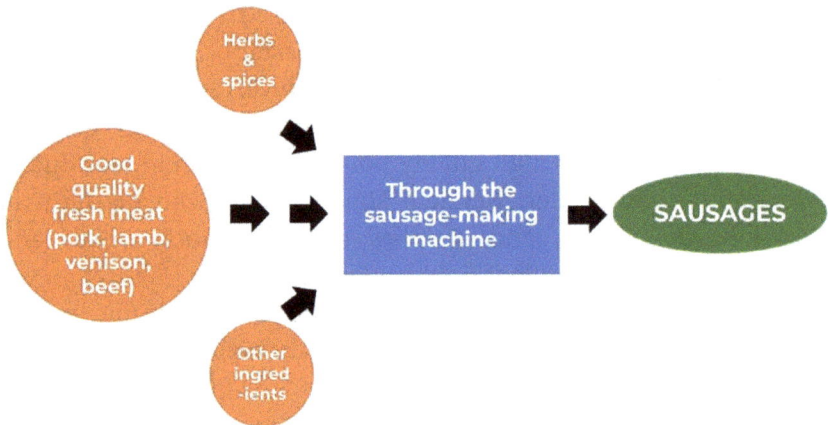

## Sausage casings

The choice of sausage casings is between natural or synthetic.

Natural casings are more expensive and can be tricky to work with. Natural casings are generally made from the intestines of the animal and are cleaned, bleached and preserved in salt and so they must be soaked in cold water before use (preferably overnight). They are the only casings that can be used in organic sausage production. Fresh casings have a shelf life of about two months if kept in salt and refrigerated. For more information, contact the International Natural Sausage Casing Association (www.insca.org).

Other casings can be vegetarian, synthetic or made from collagen. They have a much longer shelf life than natural casings and often do not need to be refrigerated. Once these casings have been filled, it is important that the sausages are left in the refrigerator overnight to rest. The herbs and spices marinate with the meat and the skins rehydrate. These skins look and feel just like normal skins, and are often less 'chewy' than fresh casings.

## The economics of making sausages

Let's consider the various stages to identify the costs and margins:

- **Supplier of raw materials:** Butcher or yourself if you have a farm;
- **Producer:** Butcher or sausage-maker;
- **Retailer:** Shop.

It is estimated that 50% to 60% of a pig carcass can be used for sausage meat, so while it's difficult to generalise, let's just say you get 25kg of sausage meat per pig and the butcher buys pigs for €25 per pig (simple figures here!), so that's €1/kg, which he sells to you at €2/kg.

| Product | Direct Costs (a) | Selling Price (b) | Simple Gross Profit (SGP) (c= b −a) | Simple Gross Margin (SGM) (d = c/bx100) |
|---------|------------------|-------------------|-------------------------------------|-----------------------------------------|
| Meat | €1 | €2 | €1 | 50% |

As the sausage-maker, you make 1.5kg of sausage from 1kg of meat, which you sell for €4.50/kg. Labour cost is not included here, but all other ingredients cost €1.

| Product | Total Direct Costs/kg (a) | Selling Price to retailer (b) | Simple Gross Profit (c= b −a) | Simple Gross Margin (d = c/bx100) |
|---------|---------------------------|-------------------------------|-------------------------------|-----------------------------------|
| Sausages | €3 | €4.50 | €1.50 | 33% |

The retailer sells the sausages for €8/kg; his/her direct cost is the purchase price s/he paid you.

| Product | Direct Costs (a) | Selling Price (b) | SGP (c = b – a) | SGM (d=c/bx100) |
|---|---|---|---|---|
| **Sausages** | €4.50 | €8 | €3.50 | 44% |

The Simple Gross Margin (SMG) in the chain shows:

- The butcher 50%;
- The sausage maker 33%;
- The shop 44%.

Margins are highest for the butcher selling just meat, then the shop-owner who sells the sausages and lowest for the sausage-maker. If the butcher makes and sells the sausages direct to the public, margins improve further. If you raise your own pigs and make the sausages yourself, then you're cutting out all the costs in the middle, but you need to consider what would be the most efficient, the easiest, and most valuable way to spend your time.

| Product | Direct Costs (a) | Selling Price (b) | SGP (c =b –a) | SGM (d = c/bx100) |
|---|---|---|---|---|
| **Sausages** | €2 | €8 | €6 | 75% |

By presenting the margins in this way, you can see at a glance where the greatest margins lie, and so the best way to make the most money. It shows clearly how a producer can add value to meat.

However, as mentioned before, the regulations around making meat products are very strict. This is not something you can do at home; you absolutely must have a dedicated premises. You will be inspected often and there is a lot of paperwork. Just know what you're getting into before you start.

# Case Study: Jane Russell's Handmade Sausages

It all began back in 1863 when Jane Russell's great-great-grandfather Edmund Burke established his pork and bacon business on O'Connell Street in Clonmel, Co. Tipperary. Jane's grandfather understood the importance of tradition and kept diaries and notebooks of all his ideas and recipes.

Almost 160 years later, Jane is proud to be carrying on this tradition (www.janerussells.ie), making a range of premium, meaty sausages by hand in Kilcullen, Co. Kildare. Jane sources all her meat from Bord Bia approved Irish farms and only uses fresh shoulder and belly meat. The oats are sourced from Flahavan's in nearby Co. Waterford.

"As we only use prime fresh cuts of Irish pork, we do not have to use strong preservatives like nitrates or nitrites, nor do we fill our packs with preserving gases", Jane says.

# Smoked Meat & Fish

If you plan to set up a smokehouse for producing smoked meat or fish, special consideration must be given to buying the unsmoked foods from a reliable (registered) source, obtaining the appropriate (microbiological) test results and ensuring that your supplier complies with all the relevant legislative and hygiene requirements.

## Cold smoking

Cold smoking is one of the oldest-known preservation methods. However, smoking of foods today is usually done for the flavour rather than for preservation. While the smoke is an anti-microbial and antioxidant, it is not sufficient for preserving food in practice, unless combined with another preservation method, such as salt-curing or drying.

Cold smoking allows total smoke penetration into the side of the meat. Very little hardening of the outside surface of the meat (casing) occurs and smoke penetrates the meat easily. Cold smoking prevents or slows down the spoilage of fats, which increases their shelf life. Cold smoked products are not submitted to any heat and so are not cooked.

Some important points to remember:

- Cold smoking is carried out typically at temperatures between 10°C and 32°C;
- Only use containers that are made from either food-grade plastic or high-quality stainless steel for preparing meats;
- Don't use woods that have been treated, or come from an unknown source;
- Using dry wood is of utmost importance when cold smoking.

Smoked salmon is smoked with cold smoke for an extended period of time. Applying hotter smoke (over 28°C) will cook the fish – sometimes sold as 'barbequed salmon' – changing the flavour and making it more difficult to slice it as thinly as the cold smoked version.

Cold smoking is a slow process. Hams, which lend themselves perfectly to this type of smoking, can be smoked from two to as long as six weeks. During smoking, they will slowly acquire a golden colour, along with a smoky flavour. You can also cold smoke salt and even sugar.

## Hot smoking

Hot smoking dries out the surface of the meat, creating a barrier for smoke penetration. Although foods that have been hot smoked are often reheated or cooked, they are typically safe to eat without further cooking. Typical temperatures used are in the range of 52°C to 80°C.

As mentioned above, an example of hot smoked fish is 'barbequed' smoked salmon, but you can also hot smoke chicken, tofu … you can try anything really!

## Food safety & other legislation

There are specific considerations to be taken into account when working with smoked fish. Listeria monocytogenes can survive at refrigeration temperatures and sometimes can be associated with food poisoning from smoked fish. The Sea Fisheries Protection Authority has produced a useful leaflet for smoked fish that can be downloaded from www.sfpa.ie. It is necessary for food producers who sell to the public to be registered with the HSE, as described in **Chapter 3**. In the UK, contact Seafish (www.seafish.org).

Specific legislation applies to the use and declaration of smoke flavourings. The Environmental Protection Agency (www.epa.ie) advises that *Air Quality Regulations* for the smoke house may apply.

## Case Study: Burren Smokehouse

The Burren Smokehouse (www.burrensmokehouse.ie) is an award-winning family-run artisan producer of smoked salmon products, set up in 1989 by Birgitta and Peter Curtin in Lisdoonvarna, Co. Clare, bringing together Scandinavian heritage and Irish history. The smokehouse supplies to high-end customers within the deli, restaurant and retail sector worldwide. All the salmon is 100% Irish and organic. Varieties include cold smoked salmon, honey-glazed cold smoked salmon with honey, whiskey and fennel (absolutely delicious!), as well as smoked salmon with seaweed, very on-trend!

The Burren Smokehouse range has been sold in the finest retail shops across the world, including Fortnum & Mason and Harrods in the UK, and Dean & Deluca in New York. You can buy it from their website, and it is widely available in Irish supermarkets and shops too and in selected stores across the UK and Europe.

A Visitor Centre was established in 1995, to create a window for Burren Smokehouse's own range and other local gourmet products and crafts. It has become a popular tourist attraction in the North County Clare area and welcomes over 30,000 visitors from all over the world each year. The Atlantic Salmon Experience is an excellent example of eco-food tourism in action, where you can immerse yourself in an interactive journey through the Atlantic waters!

# 15

# FOOD TRENDS & DEVELOPMENTS

While many new food producers continue to set up businesses, with varying levels of success, some of the most interesting are those foods which may have been niche and are now becoming more mainstream. Health and sustainability continue to influence the food market, and consumers are increasingly knowledgeable about the foods they eat, where they come from and how they impact on them and on the planet.

So, to give you some inspiration and an idea of the potential possibilities, I've selected a few examples for you to enjoy. Most of these have online shops too, if you'd like to try some and can't buy locally.

## Fermented Foods

Fermented foods are increasingly popular, both due to their taste and anecdotal health benefits. Examples include kombucha, kefir, kimchi, sauerkraut and tempeh (made from fermented cooked soya beans).

Kefir is a fermented drink that originated in the Middle East and is thought to contribute to a healthy immune system. It is traditionally made using cows or goats milk. Over a period of time, the microorganisms that are naturally present in the kefir 'grains' multiply and ferment the lactose sugars in the milk into lactic acid, so kefir tastes a bit sour, like a natural yogurt.

# Case Study: Kerry Kefir

Having long suffered from digestive issues, Mary-Thea Brosnan was prescribed tablets to be taken before every meal for the rest of her life. She spent years looking to help her symptoms through diet until a nutritionist advocated milk kefir, a fermented milk beverage packed full of beneficial bacteria and yeast. Mary-Thea sourced kefir grains and started making it herself. Within a week, the kefir had made a huge difference to her symptoms.

After 14 years in Dublin, Mary-Thea moved home to Castleisland, Co. Kerry, in October 2018 to start Kerry Kefir (www.kerrykefir.ie). She had noticed that none of the milk kefirs on the market were made in the traditional way using kefir grains but instead used powdered, lab-manufactured cultures. So Mary-Thea decided to create a premium product, using the living organisms to produce the most natural form of milk kefir as it was traditionally made, and started making it in her parents' kitchen. Mary-Thea continued to work part-time as an optometrist before taking the plunge and going full-time with Kerry Kefir in January 2020. She soon moved to a converted truck container behind the house.

Initially sold directly to customers locally and local supermarkets, Kerry Kefir has won many awards and is now available to order online for delivery nationwide, and in select health stores and independent retailers across Ireland.

"Online sales have been going so well. We are delighted. It's a great way to communicate directly with the customer, and to get a real sense of our customer retention. We also have a free packaging return programme where we take back the empty glass bottles and packaging so it can all be reused. I think many customers appreciate this, as no-one likes to throw lots of good quality packaging in the bin", says Mary-Thea.

## Food from Spent Grains

The brewing industry produces tonnes of spent grains every year, which are usually sold off cheaply as animal feed. In fact, 85% of all waste from brewing is the spent grains which remain after the wort stage. However, with more and more emphasis these days on the circular economy, sustainability and reducing food waste, opportunities to add value to these and make them into 'upcycled foods' hold great potential. For example, spent grains can be used as an ingredient in granola bars, protein snacks, or ground into flour, sprinkled on cereal, made into doggy treats, or used in functional foods.

These foods are a growing sector, and large producers include Agrain (Denmark) or Duynie (Netherlands). In Ireland, Sunkyung Choi and Patrick Nagle set up Well Spent Grains (www.well-spent-grain.com), which makes Born Again Bites, delicious vegan snacks for those on the go, for lunchboxes or any time. Another success story is BiaSol, featured below.

## Case Study: BiaSol

BiaSol (www.biasol.ie) was started in 2020 by brother and sister Niamh and Ruairi Dooley as a way to combat food waste and provide nutritious foods. Niamh is a food technologist and Ruari brought business and IT skills. Together, they have developed a range of foods that are rich in fibre and protein and can be used on their own or as an ingredient. The range includes protein pancake mix, soda bread and scone mixes, and toppings.

In the spirit of collaboration, they are always keen to work with local suppliers and brewers who are looking for better ways to deal with their spent grain. The nutrition credentials stand up, and BiaSol supplies the Irish Rugby team's chef, a great endorsement!

You can buy the BiaSol range on line and in shops and supermarkets across the country.

## 'Free-from' Food

By now, everyone is familiar with gluten-free foods. But there are so many other foods in the 'free-from' category. So many in fact, that they have their own food awards competition, imaginatively called the Free From Food Awards (www.fffa.ie)! These foods are basically allergen-free (see **Chapter 7**) and so might be nut-free, lactose-free, wheat-free, sugar-free, etc.

In July 2023, *The Grocer* published research by Kantar WorldPanel, showing that the UK market for Free From was worth £3.4bn annually, having grown in value by 8.1% over the previous 12 months, although declining in volume by 1.8%. The average price per pack across Free From has risen by 10.1%.

It is worth noting that with the exception of 'gluten-free', there is no specific UK or EU legislation covering 'free-from' health claims. Such claims, therefore, are regulated in accordance with general food law (*Regulation EC 178/2002*), as amended (see **Chapter 3**).

## Case Study: Nobó

Nobó (www.nobo.ie) was set up in 2012 by Rachel and Brian Nolan, who have been on a mission to reinvent classic treats, and create simpler, kinder, plant-based alternatives that are better for you and better for the planet, using just a few simple ingredients, sourced from the best suppliers, and as sustainably as possible but without compromising on taste. "No matter what we make, we always go back to basics and try to improve!", says Rachel.

As so many producers do, they got started from their own home kitchen in Dublin. They borrowed an ice cream machine and set off to create the perfect recipe for Frozen Goodness, Nobó's ice cream alternative. Since then the range has expanded and now includes fabulous plant-based chocolate bars and nut butter spreads. They use 100% real ingredients, and no gums, stabilisers, preservatives or additives. To make their chocolate, they combine single origin cacao with cashew nuts and coconut, to create a creamy alternative to milk chocolate with 50% less sugar.

In 2022, Brian and Rachel took the plunge with their first bricks and mortar location, expanding their team and opening their flagship store and café in Ranelagh, Dublin. Everything produced at Nobó Ranelagh is made following the same ethos and principles: 100% natural real ingredients, no refined sugar, plant-based and gluten-free. They serve locally-roasted speciality coffee, smoothies, hot chocolate and their açaí bowls which can be topped with any of their nut butters and spreads.

Nobó are continuously expanding their portfolio of foods and in 2024 they launched their first snack product: Chewy Protein Bites, clean, natural, gut-friendly and fibre-rich protein bites with 8g protein, 7g fibre and 0g refined sugar. Nobó products are widely available in shops across Ireland. You can buy them online and they also now export to Canada and Dubai!

## Restaurant to Retail

Over the years, I have worked with many restaurants and cafés who sell food to go. More specifically, some of them have turned these sales into a retail business, selling some great sauces, baked goods and curries over their own counters and through shops while continuing to run their restaurants.

When restaurants were closed during Covid-19, many chefs were forced to find alternative means of income, even in the short-term. Some of these were very successful, and the chefs never went back into the hospitality kitchen again – instead focussing on growing their new retail food businesses. One excellent example is Grainne Mullen of Grá Chocolates (www.grachocolates.com). Another is The Grill Shack Sauce Hot Sauce – below.

## Case Study: The Grill Shack Hot Sauce

Chef Aidan Kelly had been buying in hot sauce to use in his restaurant for years, but it was never quite what he was looking for and he ended up having to add ingredients to adapt it to his needs. In the end, Aidan decided it would be better if he

just made it from scratch himself, and so The Grill Shack Hot Sauce was born. Customers raved about it so much, he decided to put it into jars and sell it to them directly.

Since then, Aidan has expanded the range from his original hot sauce to now include Peri Peri and Irish Whiskey Smoked. In 2020 and 2021, The Grill Shack (www.thegrillshack.ie) hot sauces were part of the Grow with Aldi programme (www.aldi.ie/grow/) for small producers (see **Chapter 6**).

"One of the main challenges is balancing production days with restaurant opening days, but with planning and organisation it is possible", says Aidan.

## Alternative Proteins

Alternative protein is protein other than meat or fish. Alternative protein foods usually contain ingredients sourced from plants, insects, fungi (by the way, all mushrooms are fungi, but not all fungi are mushrooms), or grown in a lab (a method called tissue culture).

While still a relatively niche food group, consumers are often open to trying new foods, and if motivated by their concerns for the environment, animal welfare, or sustainability, or are simply early adopters of new technologies, then the market for these may have potential.

We have already talked about plant-based foods in **Chapter 12**. There has been quite a lot of talk about using insect protein instead of traditional meat and fish. It gets media attention, probably because of the 'ick' factor! Certainly, gaining trust and acceptance will be quite a challenge for insect protein food producers, although it is quite commonly used in aquaculture feed.

# 16

# ENGLAND, SCOTLAND, WALES & NORTHERN IRELAND

The importance of supporting local, buying local foods and food heritage is as strong in Scotland, England, Wales and Northern Ireland as it is anywhere else. There are so many traditional and unique foods:

- In **Scotland**, there is haggis, of course, and shortbread, Cullen Skink, Bannock or Cock-A-Leekie soup, or a local delicacy – the deep-fried Mars bar!
- **Wales** has its own local food, including a myriad of cheeses like Y Fenni and Perl Las. Then there is Anglesey Sea Salt, Welsh Lamb or Carmarthen ham, Conwy Mussels and Welsh laverbread (actually seaweed), Welsh rarebit, Bara Brith (a type of fruit cake), and of course, the leek, the symbol of Wales;
- **England** has even more cheese (Cheddar, Stilton, etc.), real ale, beers, clotted cream, Kendal Mint Cake, Maldon Salt, Whitstable Mussels, Yorkshire pudding, Cornish Pasties, Lancashire HotPot, Staffordshire Oatcakes – the list goes on!
- In **Northern Ireland**, there are soda farls, Yellowman (honeycomb confectionary), the Belfast Bap (great for making crisp sandwiches!), wheaten bread, Fifteens (a no-bake traybake), apples from Armagh, potato bread and champ. You might have

also come across Irish Black Butter made from apples (www.irishblackbutter.com).

Seriously though, if you're looking for local foods in any of these places, check out smaller artisan shops or take a look at recent award winners from the various competitions (see **Chapter 17**).

The artisan/speciality food and drinks sector in the UK continues to grow: in 2023, there were approximately 22,830 small and medium enterprises in the food and drink manufacturing sector, accounting for 98.8% of businesses in the sector, clearly making it a very important part of the food industry and of the economy there.

Further, the *Guardian* newspaper reported that, for every £1 spent with a small or medium-sized business, 63p stayed in the local economy, compared to 40p with a larger business.

The main trends in the UK are the same as pretty much everywhere in the Western world – sustainability, organic, veganism and vegetarianism, zero waste, innovation, local food – with, of course, the addition of the effect of Brexit. Farmers' markets, gastro pubs, and artisan food have grown considerably in popularity and quality over the past 20 years or more.

While most of the principles for starting a food business are the same no matter where you are in the world, countries differ in relation to food legislation, supports that might be available and the specifics in relation to some routes to market and so on. In addition, following Brexit, more differences are emerging as legislation starts to diverge. In this chapter, I have tried to capture and summarise as much of this as possible.

## Registration

As mentioned in **Chapter 1**, if you're a food producer in the UK, then the Food Standards Agency (www.food.gov.uk) or Food Standards Scotland (www.foodstandards.gov.scot) is the place to start looking for information. The very first thing you should do is contact the relevant section in your local authority at least 28 days before you start trading (www.food.gov.uk/here-to-help/).

If you are planning to get into hen or duck egg production, or animal slaughter and handling and/or processing meat, or fish, or making dairy products, contact your Council, which also may inspect establishments involved in animal slaughter and handling and/or processing meat. So, check out your Council website or call them to find out who you need to talk to.

The Food Standards Agency (FSA) is an independent non-ministerial Government Department. The Environmental Health Officer (EHOs) are based in the Councils and so they are your first port of call if you are thinking about starting up a new food business – see www.food.gov.uk/business-guidance/getting-ready-to-start-your-food-business/.

You must register your new business online at www.gov.uk/food-business-registration/ at least 28 days before you plan to start, and arrange for the Council to visit you to inspect and approve your kitchen and premises. The FSA website has a useful checklist for starting up, helping you think about many business issues (some of these issues are useful for any business, not just food) – see www.food.gov.uk/businessindustry/startingup/.

You don't need to be inspected or approved if you sell directly to the public or to retailers like caterers, pubs and restaurants, as long as:

* Food is less than 25% of your trade;
* You don't handle any wild game meat products;
* You don't sell food outside the county where your business is registered.

You must be inspected and approved by your local Council if your business involves handling meat, fish, egg or dairy products.

The *Safe Catering Guide* mentioned above, a *Food Start-up Guide* and all the forms you need for recording your food safety are available free at www.food.gov.uk. In Scotland, similar support is available from Food Standards Scotland (www.foodstandards.gov.scot/business-and-industry/advice-for-new-businesses/).

## Units to Rent

Food units are available across the UK for small producers that can be rented by the hour, week or longer term (try Google to find them). Agencies like CAFRE in Northern Ireland and some community and private enterprises have built proper food units finished to food production standard that you can rent – contact your local Council for more information.

In Northern Ireland, the largest Food Business Incubation Centre is situated at CAFRE's Loughry Campus (www.cafre.ac.uk) in Cookstown, Co. Tyrone. It provides eight purpose-built food processing factory units finished to the highest standards in two sizes: 175m² and 225m². The Foodovation Centre (www.foodovation.nwrc.ac.uk) at the North West Regional College in Derry has a kitchen studio and product development kitchen available to hire, along with other facilities and supports.

## Food Safety & Hygiene Legislation

In the UK, the law says that, before commencing trading, a food business operator (FBO) – that's you – must register with a competent authority – that's the Local Authority/Council office (see Registration above).

Since Brexit, UK food laws have slowly started to diverge, with new UK legislation replacing EU law piece by piece. In some cases, the EU laws were assimilated into British law. The key differences for food and feed businesses relate to how products (not just food) are traded across borders and authorisation processes for regulated products,

For food businesses in Scotland, EU legislation in relation to production, food safety, labelling, etc. continues to apply until new legislation is written (www.foodstandards.gov.scot/business-andindustry/eu-exit/). So, until all law has been changed over, producers should continue to follow EU legislation.

Having said that, the *Food Safety Act 1990* (as amended) provides the framework for all food legislation in England, Wales and Scotland. The main responsibilities for all food businesses covered by the Act are to ensure that:

- Businesses do not include anything in food, remove anything from food or treat food in any way which means it would be damaging to the health of people eating it;
- The food businesses serve or sell is of the nature, substance or quality which consumers would expect;
- The food is labelled, advertised and presented in a way that is not false or misleading.

You'll find everything you need to know on www.food.gov.uk/about-us/keyregulations/ or on www.foodstandards.gov.scot).

## The Food Hygiene Rating scheme

The scheme (https://ratings.food.gov.uk) helps you choose where to eat out or shop for food by giving you clear information about businesses' hygiene standards. It is run in partnership with local authorities in England, Wales and Northern Ireland.

*Note:* It does NOT apply to food production/manufacturing premises.

The scheme gives businesses a rating from 5 to 0 which is displayed at their premises and online so you can make more informed choices about where to buy and eat food.

> 5 – hygiene standards are very good;
>
> 4 – hygiene standards are good;
>
> 3 – hygiene standards are generally satisfactory;
>
> 2 – some improvement is necessary;
>
> 1 – major improvement is necessary;
>
> 0 – urgent improvement is required.

# Accreditation

## SALSA

SALSA (www.salsafood.co.uk) is a widely recognised food-safety standard that small food producers can adopt in order to demonstrate their compliance with food safety standards. SALSA certification is only granted to suppliers who are able to demonstrate to an auditor that they are able to produce safe and legal food and are committed to continually meeting the requirements of the SALSA standard.

SALSA accreditation can pave the way for small food producers to get listings with supermarket retailers and food service buyers, since it is a recognised food certification and provides confidence that they are producing products in safe and legal manner.

For small producers, schemes like the British Retail Consortium (BRC) are far too onerous for their businesses, so SALSA is much more suitable for their needs.

### Red Tractor

Red Tractor (www.redtractor.org.uk) is to British food and farming what the Bord Bia Quality Assurance Scheme is to producers in Ireland. The Red Tractor logo can only be used on food that has been produced, transported, stored and packed to the agreed standards of the scheme for all farming sectors (e.g., poultry, dairy or vegetables).

### British Retail Consortium Global Standards (BRCGS)

BRC (www.brcgs.com) was established by retailers who wanted to harmonise food safety standards across the supply chain. Today, BRC is globally recognised and operates one of the most rigorous third-party certification scheme of its kind.

Food producers can gain BRC accreditation for food safety, packaging materials, storage and distribution, consumer products, agents and brokers, retail, gluten-free, plant-based and ethical trading. Any producer supplying food in any volume to the large retailers will probably need BRC accreditation.

## Routes to Market

### Direct sales (B2C)

According to www.discovernorthernireland.com, there are at least nine Farmers' (outdoor) and Country (indoor) markets in Northern Ireland; www.scotlandwelcomesyou.com/scottish-farmers-markets/ shows 52 markets in Scotland; and www.welshcountry.co.uk/ farmersmarkets-in-wales/ shows 77 in Wales. It is estimated that there are about 600 in England; in London alone, there are 20 (www.lfm.org.uk) at the last count.

Online sales of artisan foods has grown considerably in the past few years and really took off during the Covid-19 pandemic, when small producers needed to find new ways to get their produce to customers. Good examples of ecommerce or online food sales in the UK for producers include the Open Food Network (www.openfoodnetwork.org.uk), and Produce & Provide (www.produceandprovide.co.uk); which is mainly for farmers. Also TheFoodMarket.com (www.thefoodmarket.com), Big Barn (www.bigbarn.co.uk), Siopio (www.siop.io), Good Sixty (www.goodsixty.co.uk), Planet Organic (www.planetorganic.com) – and, of course, there's Amazon (business.amazon.co.uk and sell.amazon.co.uk). There's Ochil Foods (www.ochilfoods.co.uk) in Scotland and The Black Mountain Smokery in Wales (www.smokedfoods.co.uk). Ocado Retail, owned by M&S, is the UK's largest on-line grocer (www.ocadoretail.com) and you can apply on-line to become a supplier at www.supplyocado.com.

IndieFude (www.indiefude.com) in Northern Ireland was the *Blas na hÉireann* Food Producers Champion in 2022 and really is a huge supporter of small producers.

There are many annual markets and fairs, Summer and Christmas food festivals (www.visitbritain.com/en/things-to-do/british-food-festivals-you-dont-want-miss/). Huge crowds attend rural Agricultural and County Shows in the UK (www.asao.co.uk/events/). In Scotland, more than 200,000 people attend the Royal Highland Show (www.royalhighlandshow.org) over four days!

## Indirect sales (B2B2C)

In the UK, Aldi, Tesco, and Sainsbury's were the most popular three supermarket chains at the end of 2023. Aldi topped the ranking with 81% of those surveyed having a positive opinion of the food retailer; Tesco and Sainsbury's came in joint second place with 79%. Having said that, Tesco and Sainsbury's have the largest actual market share when it comes to sales, followed by ASDA and Morrisons.

Producers who want to sell in Tesco must make their approach *via* its website (www.tescoplc.com/contacts/suppliers/), and not to local stores.

Lidl operates slightly differently in each country: in Northern Ireland, Lidl runs its Kick Starter programme several times a year. (www.lidl-ni.co.uk/c/kickstart/s10026058/); in the UK, you must write directly to Head Office, Lidl House, 14 Kingston Road, Surbiton, KT5 9NU with a company presentation and product information or make email contact with a Buying Manager (newsuppliers@lidl.co.uk).

You can find out how to become an Aldi supplier through its Grow with Aldi campaign; see www.aldi.co.uk/corporate/suppliers/ for details. Take note – they're very keen on suppliers with strong clean and green credentials. Aldi also has an annual competition in association with Channel 4 called Aldi's Next Big Thing (www.aldi.co.uk/next-big-thing/) which is a competition between producers to win a listing in Aldi UK.

Sainsbury's say that they are always interested in finding "innovative products that are truly unique, have an interesting heritage and, most importantly  taste great". Apply  on-line initially (www.about.sainsburys.co.uk/suppliers/becoming-a-supplier).

If you're interested in supplying Morrisons, they have two supplier programmes: Growing British Brands and Local Foodmakers – see (www.morrisons-corporate.com/suppliers/supplying-morrisons).

ASDA has partnered with RangeMe (www.rangeme.com/asda), a third-party platform that helps manage new food applications from suppliers. Register and submit your product information to the Asda buying teams on www.asdasupplier.com/becoming-a-supplier.

Iceland also has partnered with RangeMe (www.rangeme.com/icelandfoods/). Waitrose had a food producer development programme a few years ago, and is currently rebuilding it. Keep an eye on its website for information. In the meantime, food producers can approach store managers directly.

Harrods' Food Hall seeks high-performance suppliers who are able to meet its requirements for delivery, quality, responsiveness and competitiveness. In the first instance, contact the Customer Service team by email (customer.service@harrods.com) and they will forward you to the relevant buying team for consideration.

Booths has 28 stores in the North West of England and holds Meet the Buyer events every three months or so. Find out more at supply.booths.co.uk.

The Henderson Group in Northern Ireland operates Spar, Eurospar and the Vivo shops, as well as Henderson Food Service. They are very keen on local foods and stock many producers from Northern Ireland (www.henderson-group.com/supply/become-a-supplier/);

Other retailers include:

- Co-Op Food (www.coop.co.uk/our-suppliers/);
- Farmfoods UK, for frozen foods (www.farmfoods.co.uk/become-a-supplier/);
- Heron Foods (www.heronfoods.com/suppliers/);
- Oseyo, the largest Asian retailer in the UK (www.oseyo.co.uk);
- Planet Organic (www.planetorganic.com);
- Proudfoot Group, Yorkshire (www.proudfootsupermarkets.com/become-a-supplier/);
- Selfridge's Food Hall (foodbuyers@selfridges.co.uk);
- Whole Foods Market, online and stores (www.wholefoodsmarket.co.uk).

Examples of farm shops in Northern Ireland include:

- Coleman's Farm Shop, Templepatrick, Co. Antrim (www.colemansgardencentre.co.uk/farm-shop/);
- High Street Harvest, Lurgan, Co. Armagh (www.facebook.com/Highstreetharvest/);
- McKee's Country Store, Newtownards, Co. Down (www.mckeesproduce.com);
- Millar Meats, Irvinestown, Co. Fermanagh (www.facebook.com/people/Millar-Meats-Irvinestown/100051164774815/).

Then there are the independent chains (if that's not a contradiction in terms!), such as Premier (www.premier-stores.co.uk), Budgens (www.budgens.co.uk/about-us/) or Nisa (www.nisalocally.co.uk).

You also could exhibit at the annual Speciality Food Fair in London (www.specialityandfinefoodfairs.co.uk) or at the Natural Food Expo (www.naturalfoodexpo.co.uk) or any of the many trade shows and try to meet supermarket buyers in the UK that way. You can download our lists of trade shows at www.alphaomega.ie/shop/.

There is more about how to prepare for meeting supermarket buyers in **Chapter 6**.

## Other routes

In Scotland, the Supplier Development Programme is a collaboration between the councils, and runs annually helping suppliers win public tender contracts (worth £14.5 billion) across all sectors (www.sdpscotland.co.uk/about/). It might be worth checking out.

Showcasing Scotland is organised by Scotland Food & Drink on behalf of the Scotland Food & Drink Partnership with support from the Scottish Government. The event in 2024 welcomed over 100 of the world's most influential food and drink buyers to conduct 1,822 official meetings with over 100 Scottish exporting or export-ready food and drink businesses (www.foodanddrink.scot).

Business Wales runs several Trade Development programmes (see businesswales.gov.wales/foodanddrink/growing-your-business/trade-development-programme/).

## Exporting to the EU

Since Brexit, exporting to the EU has become more difficult in terms of paperwork and compliance with customs.

Exporting from Northern Ireland into the Republic is covered under separate legislation (the Windsor Framework). Sending goods across the Irish Sea into Northern Ireland from GB has another set of rules, some of which come into force on a phased basis.

It's all still a movable feast, so for updates, keep an eye on UK Government websites (www.gov.uk/government/collections/the-windsor-framework-further-detail-and-publications/).

For up-to-date information on exporting goods from GB to the EU, see www.gov.uk/export-goods/.

## Food Tourism

Food tourism experiences abound all across Northern Ireland and Great Britain. You can find everything from chocolate-making, whiskey-tasting, bread-baking, pie-making, fermenting or foraging – and even visit a vineyard. Fabulous markets like St. George's Market in Belfast (www.belfastcity.gov.uk/stgeorgesmarket/) or Borough Market (www.boroughmarket.org.uk) in London are worth a trip.

## Case Study: Sussex Vineyards

Sussex is England's wine homeland (www.sussexmodern.org.uk/wine/). From West Sussex to East Sussex, a new generation of winemakers is rapidly growing the industry, receiving international acclaim and putting English wine firmly on the global map. You can visit 17 of these vineyards, and can reach three of the Eastbourne vineyards by bike if you're feeling energetic! You can drive yourself on a self-guided tour or hop on a bus and let someone else be the designated driver! See Great British Wine Tours (www.greatbritishwinetours.co.uk/sussex-wine-routes/).

On a visit, you'll meet the winemaker, hear all about how the wine is made, the regenerative practices used by some, and its unique flavours – and taste the wine, of course,

## Branding & Patents

Talk to the Patents Office (www.gov.uk/government/organisations/intellectual-property-office/) for information about protecting your brand name, trademark and/or logo.

### *Protected Geographical Indicator in the UK*

The UK Geographical Indicator (GI) schemes protect registered product names when they are sold in Great Britain (England, Scotland and Wales). Some examples of these include Gower Marsh Lamb, Beacon Fell Traditional Leicester Cheese, and Scottish Farmed Salmon.

The EU GI schemes protect registered products names when they are sold in Northern Ireland and the EU.

What about Brexit? Well, all product names protected in the EU on 31 December 2020, following successful applications to the EU GI schemes, are still protected under both UK and EU GI schemes.

There are four different GI schemes operating in the UK depending on your product type:

- Protected Food Name (PFN) for food, agricultural products, beer, cider and perry;

- Either a PDO or PGI for wine;
- Either PDO or PGI for aromatised wines;
- Protected Spirit Drink Names (PSDN) for, you've guessed it, spirit drinks.

There is also protection for Traditional Name Terms, which is a mark for distinctiveness or quality for wines – Quality Sparking wine and Regional Sparking wine, for example.

Some foods are protected under the Traditional Speciality Guaranteed (TSG), including Traditional Bramley Apple filling, watercress, and Traditionally Farmed Gloucestershire Old Spots Pork.

Producers in Great Britain must successfully apply for the UK GI schemes before applying to the EU schemes to protect a product name in Northern Ireland or the EU.

For more information or application forms etc, go to www.gov.uk/guidance/protect-a-geographical-food-or-drink-name-in-the-uk/ for details.

# Food Awards & Competitions

Entering your food product into any of the many food awards and competitions is a great way to get free promotion and PR for you and your food business.

The big competitions in the UK are the Great Taste Awards (www.greattasteawards.co.uk) and the Quality Food Awards (uk.qualityfoodawards.com). In addition, UK producers who sell their foods in Ireland are also eligible to enter the Irish Quality Food & Drink Awards (irish.qualityfoodawards.com). Scotland has the Scotland Food & Drink Excellence Awards (www.excellenceawards.foodanddrink.scot), as well as the Highlands & Islands Food & Drink Awards (www.hifoodanddrinkawards.com) and the North East Scotland Food & Drink Awards (www.nesfoodanddrinkawards.co.uk).

See more in the list in **Chapter 17**.

## Food Labelling

Requirements for labelling on food in the UK (www.gov.uk/foodlabelling-and-packaging/food-labelling-what-you-must-show/) is very similar to that in the EU and until new UK legislation is written, the EU law applies. Your label must show:

- The name of the food;
- A 'best before' or 'use by' date;
- Any necessary warnings (some specific types of ingredients have specific warnings – for example, aspartame, polyols, raw milk and others);
- Net quantity information;
- A list of ingredients (if there is more than one) – allergens to be highlighted and QUID (the quantity of certain ingredients) applies;
- The country or place of origin, if required;
- The lot number or use-by date;
- Any special storage conditions;
- Instructions for use or cooking, if necessary.

If you're selling food in Great Britain (England, Wales and Scotland), you must also include the name and address of the UK or EU business responsible for the information on the food. If the business is not in the UK or EU, you must include the name and address of the importer.

If you're selling food in Northern Ireland, you must include the name and address of the Northern Irish or EU business responsible for the information on the food. If the business is not in Northern Ireland or the EU, you must include the name and address of the importer.

### Allergens

'Natasha's Law' is a new allergen labelling law in force since 2021 that affects prepacked for direct sale (PPDS) foods in the UK. The changes to food labelling laws affect businesses in Northern Ireland that package and sell or offer foods on-site to the final customer. You can find information about how to implement the requirements of the law in your business on www.Safefood.net/allergens/natashas-law/.

Information about allergen labelling generally can be found on the Food Standards Agency's website: www.food.gov.uk/business-guidance/allergen-guidance-for-food-businesses/.

## Nutrition labelling

It is compulsory for food producers to declare nutrition information on prepacked food. The FSA is responsible for nutrition labelling (www.food.gov.uk/business-guidance/nutrition-labelling/).

District Councils enforce these regulations in Northern Ireland.

## Organic labelling

As in the EU, there are strict rules around the use of the term 'organic' when it comes to food (www.gov.uk/guidance/organic-food-labelling-rules/). You are breaking the law if you call a food product 'organic' if it has not been inspected and certified.

You can only label food as 'organic', or use terms relating to organic production methods, if:

- It meets organic production rules;
- At least 95% of the agricultural ingredients are organic;
- All other ingredients, additives and processing aids are listed as permitted within the organic regulations;
- The product, its labels and any suppliers are certified by an approved UK organic control body.

Other terms relating to organic methods include:

- 'Organically grown';
- 'Organically produced';
- 'Grown or produced using organic principles';
- 'Grown or produced using organic methods'.

The rules also apply to company names or brand names. For example, you could not use the name 'Smith's Organic' for a non-organic product or business.

Organic labelling includes requirements for displaying the organic certification license number, the symbol of the particular certification body with whom you are registered, as well as all the standard stuff.

## *Gluten-free labelling*

For details on using the internationally recognised Crossed Grain symbol or information on how you can cater better to the gluten-free consumer, contact Coeliac UK (www.coeliac.org.uk/food-businesses/) for information for the hospitality sector, retailers and food producers.

Contamination during the baking process is a major hazard in a kitchen since your 'gluten-free' food can easily be contaminated with gluten from your other foods. Control here is critical and you really must get advice from your EHO or Inspector and from Coeliac UK about your set-up.

# Sources of Finance, Funding & Supports

As a starting point, you should visit the Food Standards Agency food business support hub at www.food.gov.uk/here-to-help/.

Your local Councils and Enterprise Agencies may have funding to help you with feasibility studies, training or equipment.

Rural Development Programmes for England, Scotland, Northern Ireland and Wales provide funding to improve agriculture, the environment and rural life. For more information, see www.gov.uk/rural-development-programme-for-england/ or www.daera-ni.gov.uk/topics/rural-development/rural-development-programme/.

In addition, they usually have a list of experienced mentors with specialisms in food, finance, business start-up and more that you can access, often for free, but certainly for a small percentage of the actual cost. The Enterprise Agencies also may provide funding for attendance at trade shows.

Invest Northern Ireland (www.investni.com) offers a range of funding support to food and drink businesses including the Innovation Vouchers scheme (www.investni.com/support-for-business/innovation-research-and-development/innovation-vouchers/), which is open to food businesses that are registered companies. Sole traders are generally not eligible but sometimes the scheme is opened to sole traders or artisan producers, so keep an eye out for it. My advice is to choose your knowledge partner carefully, ask them for a work plan, dates for completion and find out who exactly will be working on your project with you.

Check out all Invest NI's supports (www.investni.com/support-forbusiness/), which include international trade missions, exhibitions, R&D funding, IP assistance and more.

The Department of Agriculture, Environment & Rural Affairs (DAERA) in Northern Ireland has funding available at various times of the year for food producers and farmers (www.daera-ni.gov.uk/grants-and-funding/food-grants/). This includes the Northern Ireland Regional Food Programme (www.daera-ni.gov.uk/articles/northern-ireland-regionalfood-programme/). Keep an eye on the DAERA website for funding calls.

For up-to-date information, check NI Business Info (www.nibusinessinfo.co.uk/business-support/).

Inter*Trade*Ireland (www.intertradeireland.com) offers supports and information for businesses across the whole island of Ireland (see **Chapter 6**).

And across the UK, there is advice and support from a number of schemes (see www.gov.uk/business-support-helpline/), while locally, you may find other funding opportunities. For example, in Buckinghamshire, there is a business support network for rural businesses called Rural Ngage (bbf.uk.com/rural-ngage/).

## Insurance for Trading

As mentioned previously, it is wise to take out both product liability and public liability insurance once you start selling your food. If you employ staff, then you'll need employer's liability too, and there may be other insurances to consider, including product recall insurance.

In the UK, try Mobilers Insurance Services (www.mobilers.co.uk) – and there are many others. It might be best to contact an insurance broker to make sure you get a few quotes.

## Training

Ask your Local Council for information about courses for small businesses generally. Some food skills training providers include:

- CAFRE (NI): Lots of courses, everything from cheese-making to train the trainer and more (www.cafre.ac.uk);
- The Food Standards Agency: A really good elearning programme for food labelling (www.labellingtraining.food.gov.uk).

## Case Study: Rora Dairy

On an organic farm in Aberdeenshire, with a herd of over 250 dairy cows, three different types of natural yogurt are made from their fresh unhomogenised milk. The yogurts are high in protein and contain four different strains of live bacteria. Rora Dairy (www.roradairy.co.uk) was founded and is run by Jane Mackie, who has added flavoured varieties now too.

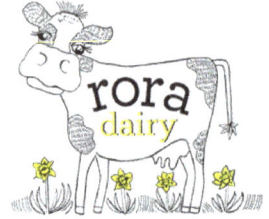

Sustainability is a top priority here. The farm has a wind turbine and solar panels to produce electricity; wildlife corridors enable wildlife to travel safely between the streams, rivers and woodlands; and the seven new woods and copses, along with several kilometres of new hedges around the farm, have become home to many creatures, including black birds, woodcock, corn bunting, thrush, roe deer, foxes and mice.

Rora yogurts are available throughout Scotland in Sainsbury's, Co-op and Asda as well as lots of independent, artisan shops across the UK.

## Case Study: Conwy Kombucha

Started in 2018, Conwy Kombucha is a multi-award-winning, family-owned business. They are passionate about Kombucha and their search for the authentic, traditional experience led the family to making their own – a familiar tale!

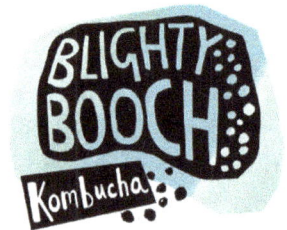

Their high-quality organic Blighty Booch Kombucha (www.blightybooch.com) is made in their SALSA, OF&G Organic, and Vegan certified premises using a natural and authentic method of production.

The kombucha is naturally carbonated, providing a rich array of antioxidants, polyphenols, and other beneficial bioactive compounds that are produced during the fermentation process. The Organic Ginger Kombucha was recognised as a Top 50 product out of 12,700 entries in the 2020 Great Taste Awards.

Conwy Kombucha also offer make-at-home Blighty Baby kit ranges and a selection of organic loose-leaf teas, which is a great way to give line-extensions and increase the range of products for sale to consumers.

In 2020, Blighty Brew Whole-leaf Tea was launched, a range of Organic Green and Black Teas. In 2023, they won Artisan Producer of the Year at the Welsh Food & Drink Awards. Every bottle of their Blighty Booch Kombucha has 'Made in Wales' proudly printed on the label. *Iechyd da pawb!*

## Case Study: Lough Neagh Eels

The tradition of eating of eel in the Neagh-Bann region dates back to the earliest arrival of humans in Northern Ireland at Mount Sandel, Coleraine, 9,000 years ago. As long ago as the 6th century, monks set eel traps in the lough, using lines as long as six miles with hundreds of individually baited hooks. For centuries, the Lough Neagh fisheries were under the control of the great Gaelic chieftains before passing to various aristocrats but, in the early 1960s, local priest Father Oliver Kennedy began a long battle to win the rights for a co-operative of local fishermen (www.loughneagheels.com) who used traditional methods to catch eels.

Around Lough Neagh, there is a wonderful culture of eating fried eel, known locally as 'eel suppers'. However, the majority of eel caught in Lough Neagh is sent to Holland (for smoking) and Great Britain. In the East End of London, Lough Neagh Eel is used in the production of jellied eel, a traditional English dish that originated in the 18th century. It is also growing in popularity in high-end restaurants and fine-dining across Northern Ireland.

The award of Protected Geographical Indication (PGI) provided by EU law in 2011 to 'Lough Neagh Eel' is regarded by the local industry as a significant accolade, recognising the heritage, tradition and authenticity of what are regarded as the best quality eel available in Europe.

## M's Bakery

M's (www.msbakery.co.uk) is an award winning, family-run artisan bakery which started as many often do – baking at home and selling through the local market. They now have two stores: one in Bournemouth and the other in nearby Christchurch in the South of England.

Everything is made from scratch right on the premises, using local ingredients where possible and without using any artificial ingredients. Quality is a top priority and each pastry and bread has a total of three days of hard work behind it.

M's sourdough bread won Overall Gold in the World Bread Awards (www.worldbreadawards.com) in both 2018 and 2022. Made using traditional methods, each load of M's sourdough takes at least 24 hours to make, from building a starter to baking the loaf.

# 17

# KEY RESOURCES & SOURCES OF INFORMATION

Many resources and sources of information have been mentioned throughout the book. Here they are again, all in one place – plus a few more.

## Bakery Supplies

Andrews Food Ingredients (www.andrewsingredients.co.uk)
Bakery Bits Ltd (www.bakerybits.co.uk)
Easy Equipment – for wicker bread baskets (www.easyequipment.ie)
G&S Services Bakery Equipment Ltd (www.gandsbakeryequipment.co.uk)
McGrath Bakery Services Ltd – new & used equipment
    (www.mcgrathbakeryservices.com)
Rademaker BV (Netherlands) (www.rademaker.com)
Scobie Bakery – for when you go big time! (www.scobiebakery.com)
Stratton Sales & Service (USA) (www.strattonsales.com)

## Books

*Bord Bia Foodservice Directory* (www.bordbia.info/Foodservices-2023/)
*Bread Science* / Emily Buehler
*Dairy Microbiology* / RK Robinson (1981) – an old text, but regarded as the definitive guide
*Facebook Marketing* / Louise McDonnell / The Liffey Press
*Flying Off the Shelves: The Food Entrepreneur's Guide to Selling* / Tessa Stuart
*Food Throughout the Ages* / Prof. Mike Gibney

*Manufacturing Yogurt & Fermented Milks* / RC Chandan / Wiley-Blackwell
*Microbiology & Technology of Fermented Foods* (2006) / RW Hutkins
*Packed: The Food Entrepreneur's Guide: How to Get Noticed & How to Be Loved* / Tessa Stuart
*Practical Poultry* magazine (www.practicalpoultry.co.uk)
*Starting a Business in Ireland* (2023, 8e) / Brian O'Kane / Oak Tree Press (www.successstore.com)
*Starting Your Own Business: A Workbook* (2024, 5e) / Ron Immink & Brian O'Kane / Oak Tree Press (www.successstore.com)
*The Composition of Foods* / McCance & Widdowson / Royal Society of Chemistry
*The Sausage Book* / Paul Peacock / Kitchen Newbie

## Dairy Suppliers
DairyCo (Ukraine) (www.dairyco.com.ua)
Goat Nutrition Ltd (www.gnltd.co.uk)

### Cheese
ALPMA GB Ltd (www.alpma.co.uk)
C. van't Riet Dairy Technology BV (Netherlands) (www.rietdairy.nl/en/)
Jongia (Netherlands) (www.jongia.com)
Rademaker BV (Netherlands) (www.rademaker.com)
Specialist Cheesemakers Association (www.specialistcheesemakers.co.uk)
Stratton Sales & Service (USA) (www.strattonsales.com)

### Ice cream
Alfred & Co. (www.alfredandco.com)
Ashwood Trade Products (UK) (www.ashwood.biz)
Carpigiani UK Ltd (www.carpigiani.co.uk)
Cater Link (www.caterlink.co.uk)
Dairyglen (www.dairyglen.ie)
RSS Ltd (www.rsshereford.co.uk)

## Food Awards & Competitions
*Blas na hÉireann*/National Irish Food Awards (www.irishfoodawards.com)
British Cheese Awards (www.britishcheeseawards.com)
European Private Label Awards (www.privatelabelawards.com)
Euro-toques Food Awards (www.euro-toques.ie/food-awards-2/)
Free From Food Awards (www.freefromfoodawards.co.uk)
Free From Food Awards Ireland (www.fffa.ie)
Good Food Ireland Awards (www.goodfoodireland.ie)

Great British Food Awards (www.greatbritishfoodawards.com)
Great Taste Awards, Guild of Fine Food (www.gff.co.uk/for-
    producers/great-taste/)
Green Food & Beverage Producer Awards (www.gfba.ie)
Highlands & Islands Food & Drink Awards
    (www.hifoodanddrinkawards.com)
Irish Food Writers Guild Awards (www.irishfoodwritersguild.ie/food-
    awards/)
Irish Quality Food & Drink Awards (irish.qualityfoodawards.com)
Northern Ireland Food & Drink Association (www.nifda.co.uk/awards/)
North East Scotland Food & Drink Awards
    (www.nesfoodanddrinkawards.co.uk)
Quality Food Awards (www.qualityfoodawards.com)
Retail Industry Awards (UK) (www.retailindustryawards.com)
Scotland Food & Drink Excellence Awards
    (www.excellenceawards.foodanddrink.scot)
Wales Food & Drink Awards (www.foodanddrinkawards.wales)
World Bread Awards (www.worldbreadawards.com)
World Cheese Awards (www.gff.co.uk/for-producers/worldcheese-awards/)
World Drinks Awards – beer, cider, wine, spirits
    (www.worlddrinksawards.com)
World Steak Challenge (www.worldsteakchallenge.com)

# Funding & Support Agencies

*Ireland*
Bord Bia (www.bordbia.ie)
Department of Agriculture, Food & the Marine (DAFM)
    (www.agriculture.gov.ie)
Department of Enterprise, Trade & Employment
    (https://supportingsmes.gov.ie)
EIT Food (www.eitfood.eu)
Enterprise Ireland (www.enterprise-ireland.com/en/)
Environmental Protection Agency – Stop Food Waste (www.epa.ie)
Euro-toques (www.euro-toques.ie)
Fáilte Ireland – for food tourism (www.failteireland.ie/foodtourism.aspx)
Food Safety Authority of Ireland (www.fsai.ie)
Health Service Executive/Environmental Health Officers, (www.hse.ie/
    eng/services/list/1/environ/environmental-health-officers.html)
Innovation Vouchers (Enterprise Ireland) (www.innovationvouchers.ie)
Inter*Trade*Ireland (www.intertradeireland.com)
Local Authority Veterinary Services (www.fsai.ie/business-advice/
    starting-a-food-business/register/local-authority-contact-details/)

Local Enterprise Offices (www.localenterprise.ie)
MicroFinance Ireland (www.microfinanceireland.ie)
National Dairy Council (www.ndc.ie)
Rural Development Companies/Irish Local Development Network
    (www.ildn.ie/themes/urban-and-rural-development/)
Sea Fisheries Protection Authority (www.sfpa.ie)
Teagasc (www.teagasc.ie)
Údarás na Gaeltachta (www.udaras.ie)

## UK
Agriculture & Horticulture Development Board (www.ahdb.org.uk)
Business Durham (www.businessdurham.co.uk)
Campden BRI (www.campdenbri.co.uk)
Dairy UK (www.dairyuk.org)
Department for Business & Trade (UK) – UK Export Academy
    (www.great.gov.uk)
Enterprise Revolution (Tees Valley) (www.enterpriserevolution.co.uk)
Food & Drink Exporters Association (UK) (www.ukfdea.com)
Food Standards Scotland (www.foodstandards.gov.scot)
Leatherhead Food Research (www.leatherheadfood.com)
National Enterprise Network (www.nationalenterprisenetwork.org)
Research & Innovation/Innovate UK (www.ukri.org)
Start & Grow (www.startandgrowuk.org)
TEDCO (North East of England) (www.tedco.org)
UK importing from EU (including Ireland) into the UK
    (www.gov.ie/en/publication/668a0-uk-import-controls-2023-the-
    border-target-operating-model-tom/)

## England
Business Support Helpline (www.gov.uk/business-support-helpline)
Food & Drink Federation (www.fdf.org.uk)
Fresh Produce Consortium (www.freshproduce.org.uk)
Innovate UK (www.iuk.ktn-uk.org)
Small Business (www.smallbusiness.co.uk)

## Northern Ireland
College of Agriculture, Food & Rural Enterprise (www.cafre.ac.uk)
Department of Agriculture, Environment & Rural Affairs (www.daera-
    ni.gov.uk/topics/ruraldevelopment/rural-development-programme/)
Enterprise Causeway (www.enterprisecauseway.co.uk)
Enterprise NI (www.enterpriseni.com/councils)
Food Business Incubation Centre – CAFRE (www.cafre.ac.uk)
Food Standards Agency Northern Ireland (www.food.gov.uk/northern-
    ireland/)

Inter*Trade*Ireland (www.intertradeireland.com)
Invest Northern Ireland (www.investni.com)
NI Business Info (www.nibusinessinfo.co.uk)

### Scotland

Arran's Food Journey (www.arransfoodjourney.com)
Ayrshire Food an' a' That (www.ayrshirefood.org)
East Lothian Food & Drink (www.scotlandsfooddrinkcounty.com)
Eat & Visit SW Scotland (www.facebook.com/eatswscotland)
Food Standards Scotland (www.foodstandards.gov.scot)
Interface – connecting academics and industry
    (www.interfaceonline.org.uk/funding/)
Lanarkshire Larder (www.lanarkshirelarder.com)
Scotland Food & Drink (www.foodanddrink.scot)
Scottish Rural Development Programme (SRDP) (www.ruralpayments.org/
    topics/all-schemes/food-processing-marketing-and-co-operation/)
Seafood Scotland (www.seafoodscotland.org)
Slow Food Scotland (www.slowfoodscotland.com)

### Wales

Food & Drink Wales (www.food-drink.wales)
Food & Drink Wales Cluster Network (www.businesswales.gov.wales/
    foodanddrink/growing-your-business/clusters/)
Food Innovation Wales (www.foodinnovation.wales)

## General Equipment Suppliers

Buy & Sell – lists second-hand equipment for sale (www.buyandsell.ie)
DoneDeal – lists second-hand equipment and ice cream carts for sale
    (www.donedeal.ie)
Ebay – many commercial machines listed for sale (www.ebay.ie)
Fullwood Packo (www.fullwoodjoz.com/uk/)
Gumtree (www.gumtree.com)
Jongia (Netherlands) (www.jongia.com)
Martin Food Equipment (www.martinfoodequip.com)
Nisbets – supply both domestic and small commercial scale equipment
    (www.nisbets.ie)
Robot Coupe (www.robotcoupe.co.uk)

## Gluten-free

Coeliac Society of Ireland (www.coeliac.ie)
Coeliac UK (www.coeliac.org.uk/home/)

## Kitchen/Production Space to Rent

A list for Ireland and Northern Ireland can be downloaded free from www.alphaomega.ie/product/rent-kitchen-space/.

## Local Food Networks & Producer Groups

Formal Producer Organisations or POs can be defined as legally constituted groups of producers or farmers (EU Commission, 2017). Most food and drink networks are not formalised in this way, however, and there are almost too many to include, so here is just a selection.

*Ireland*
Boyne Valley Flavours (www.boynevalleyflavours.ie)
Cáis – Association of Irish Cheese-makers (www.irishcheese.ie)
County Dublin Beekeepers' Association (www.dublinbees.org)
Created in Cavan (www.createdincavan.ie)
Donegal Food Coast (www.donegalfoodcoast.ie/map/)
Dublin Food Chain (www.dublinfoodchain.ie)
Federation of Irish Beekeepers' Associations (www.irishbeekeeping.ie)
Laois Taste (www.laoistaste.ie)
Love Irish Food (www.loveirishfood.ie)
Mayo Food & Drink (www.mayofood.ie/Food Coast Donegal/)
Midlands Ireland (www.midlandsireland.ie/business/food-and-drink-cluster/)
Sligo Food Trail (www.sligofoodtrail.ie/producers/)
Slow Food Ireland (www.slowfoodireland.com)
Taste Cork (www.tastecork.ie)
Taste Kerry (www.tastekerry.ie)
Taste Leitrim (www.tasteleitrim.com)
Taste Waterford (www.tastewaterford.ie)
Tipperary Food Producers (www.tipperaryfoodproducers.ie)
Wexford Food Family (www.wexfordfoodfamily.com)
Wicklow Naturally (www.wicklownaturally.ie)

*UK*
Advanced Food & Drink Manufacturing Network (NI) (www.www.afdmnetwork.com)
Bee Farmers Association (www.beefarmers.co.uk)
Bristol Food Producers (www.bristolfoodproducers.uk)
Campaign for Real Ale (www1.camra.org.uk)
Cotswold Taste (www.cotswoldtaste.co.uk)
Deliciously Yorkshire (www.deliciouslyorkshire.co.uk)
Dorset Food & Drink (www.dorsetfoodanddrink.org)

Eat Sleep Live Herefordshire (www.eatsleepliveherefordshire.co.uk)
Food & Drink Federation (www.fdf.org.uk)
Food & Drink Forum (www.foodanddrinkforum.co.uk)
Food & Drink North East (www.fadne.org)
Food Drink Devon (www.fooddrinkdevon.co.uk)
Food from England (www.foodfromengland.co.uk)
Greater Lincolnshire Local Enterprise Partnership
    (www.greaterlincolnshirelep.co.uk)
Guild of Fine Food (www.gff.co.uk)
Hampshire Fare (www.hampshirefare.co.uk)
London Butchers (www.londonbutchers.org.uk)
Made in Derbyshire (www.madeinderbyshire.org)
Made in Northamptonshire (www.madeinnorthamptonshire.org)
National Association of Cider Makers (www.cideruk.com)
Produced in Kent (www.producedinkent.co.uk)
Raw Milk Producers Association (www.rawmilkproducers.co.uk)
Shropshire Food & Drink (www.shropshirefoodanddrink.co.uk)
Slow Food (www.slowfood.org.uk)
Specialist Cheesemakers Association (www.specialistcheesemakers.co.uk)
Sussex Food & Drink (www.sussexfoodanddrink.org)
Taste Cheshire (www.tastecheshire.com)
Taste of the West (www.tasteofthewest.co.uk)
The Ice Cream Alliance (UK) (www.ice-cream.org)
Welsh Food & Drink (www.welshfoodanddrink.wales)

*Northern Ireland*
Institute of Northern Ireland Beekeepers (www.inibeekeepers.com)
NI Good Food/Taste of Ulster (www.nigoodfood.com)
Northern Ireland Food & Drink Association (NIFDA) (www.nifda.co.uk)
Slow Food NI (www.slowfood.org.uk/slow-food-northernireland/)
Taste Causeway (www.tastecauseway.com)
Ulster Beekeepers Association (www.ubka.org)

# Meat Sector Suppliers

Brennan Group (www.brennan-group.com)
CF Gaynor Ltd – for marinades, sauces, herbs and spices, sausage mixes
    and coatings (www.cfgaynor.com)
International Natural Sausage Casing Association (www.insca.org)
Irish Casing Company Ltd – for casings (www.irishcasings.com)
McDonnell's Ltd (www.mcdonnells.ie)
ProQ Smokers (www.proqsmokers.co.uk)
Scobie & Junor (Dublin) Ltd (www.scobiesdirect.com)

## Packaging

A list of packaging suppliers can be downloaded free from the Shop page on www.alphaomega.ie.

## Patents/Intellectual Property/Brand protection

Intellectual Property Office (UK) (www.ipo.gov.uk)
Patents Office (www.patentsoffice.ie)

## Sensory Analysis Services

AFBI, Belfast (www.afbini.gov.uk/contacts/sensory-evaluation-unit/)
ALS Testing (UK) (www.als-testing.co.uk/services/consultancy-training/)
Amárach Research, Dublin (www.amarach.com/seven-reasons/ food-sensory-panels.html)
ATU, Galway (www.atu.ie)
College of Agriculture, Food & Rural Enterprise (NI) (www.cafre.ac.uk)
Campden BRI (UK) (www.campdenbri.co.uk/consumer-sensory-courses.php)
Eolas International, Cork (www.eolasinternational.com)
Harper Adams University (www.harper-adams.ac.uk/work-with-us/)
Innovate Solutions, Dublin (www.innovatesolutions.ie)
MMR Consumer Research (UK) (www.mmr-research.com)
SenseLab (UK) (www.sense-lab.co.uk/sensory-testing-facility/)
SRL Pharma, Cork (www.srlpharmasenses.com/services/)
Synergy Flavours (UK) (www.uk.synergytaste.com)
Teagasc, Dublin (www.teagasc.ie)
The Research Suite, Drogheda
    (sites.google.com/view/theresearchsuite/)
TU Dublin, Grangegorman (www.tudublin.ie)
TUS, Limerick (www.lit.ie)
UCC, Cork (www.ucc.ie)
UCD, Dublin (www.ucd.ie)
Ulster University, Coleraine (www.ulster.ac.uk)
Wirral Sensory Services (UK) (www.wssintl.com)

## Sustainability

B-Corp (www.bcorporation.net/en-us/)
B-Lab Europe/B-Lab UK (www.bcorporation.eu)
Bord Bia Origin Green (www.origingreen.ie)

Business Working Responsibly Mark (www.nsai.ie/certification/
     management-systems/business-working-responsibly-mark/)
ENSO Initiatives (www.ensoimpact.com)
EPA Food Waste Charter (www.foodwastecharter.ie)
Love Food Hate Waste (www.lovefoodhatewaste.com)
REPAK (www.repak.ie)
Stop Food Waste (www.stopfoodwaste.ie)
United Nations Sustainable Development Goals (SDGs)
     (www.sdgs.un.org/goals/)
WRAP (www.wrap.org.uk)

# Training

As well as short courses from the support and funding agencies listed above, and from both private and other providers, most Universities and Colleges of Further Education offer food science, food technology, food production, environmental and sustainability courses, ranging from certificates to post-graduate degrees.

## Butchery training

Associated Craft Butchers of Ireland – National Butchery Apprenticeship
     (www.craftbutchers.ie)
Regan Organic Farm (www.reganorganicfarm.ie)
Smokin' Soul (www.smokinsoul.ie/butchery/)

## Dairy training

Academy of Cheese (UK) (www.academyofcheese.org)
Broughgammon Farm (NI) (www.broughgammon.com/events/)

## Food hygiene & HACCP training providers

About Hygiene Ltd – on-line and in-person courses in Ireland
     (www.about-hygiene.com)
Environmental Health Association of Ireland (www.ehai.ie/courses/)
Food Flow Advisors (www.foodflow.ie)
safefood – free Level 1 Food Hygiene Training
     (www.safefood.net/safefood-for-business/)
SALSA (www.salsafood.co.uk)
The Food Safety Company, Dublin & Cork
     (www.thefoodsafetycompany.ie)

## General, food hygiene & sector-specific training

Ballymaloe Cookery School – courses from half-day to 12 weeks
     (www.ballymaloecookeryschool.ie)

British Retail Consortium (BRCGS) (www.brcgs.com/training/e-
    learning/)
College of Agriculture, Food & Rural Enterprise (NI) (www.cafre.ac.uk)
Campden BRI (UK) (www.campdenbri.co.uk)
Food Industry Training Unit, UCC (www.ucc.ie/fitu/)
Leatherhead Food Research (UK) (www.leatherheadfood.com)
National Organic Training Skillnet – open to non-organic producers also
    (www.nots.ie)
SALSA (www.salsafood.co.uk/shared/index.php?p=17/)
School of Artisan Food (UK) – baking, cheesemaking, brewing, butchery,
    etc. (www.schoolofartisanfood.org)
Scottish Funding Council (www.sfc.ac.uk)
Skillnet (www.skillnetireland.ie)
Taste 4 Success Skillnet (www.taste4success.ie)
Teagasc, Moorepark Food Research Centre, Fermoy (www.teagasc.ie)
The Organic Centre (www.theorganiccentre.ie)

### Ice cream-making courses
Carpigiani UK Ltd – an Italian ice cream equipment manufacturer,
    providing high quality equipment and services, which runs ice cream-
    making courses in Bologna and the UK (www.gelatouniversity.com)
RSS Ltd – *Introduction to Artisan Ice Cream and Fruit Ice*
    (www.rsshereford.co.uk)
The Ice Cream Alliance (UK) (www.ice-cream.org)

### Producers offering cheese-making courses
Knockdrinna – a one-day cheese-making course where you make your own
    cheese in the morning, enjoy lunch and then take your handmade creation
    home for maturing. For those in the catering industry or interested in food
    production for a living, Helen Finnegan is currently designing a
    professional cheese-making guidance course (www.knockdrinna.com)
Moorlands Cheesemakers – a great list of cheese courses across the UK
    (www.cheesemaking.co.uk)

## Other Useful Contacts
Aldi (www.aldi.ie)
Avoca (www.avoca.com)
BIS Research (www.bisresearch.com)
Blenders (www.blenders.ie)
Brandshapers Ltd. (www.brandshapers.ie)
Cloverhill Food Ingredients Ltd (www.cloverhill.ie)
Curran Foods (www.curranfoods.ie)
Food Works (www.foodworksireland.ie)

Fresh the Good Food Market (www.freshthegoodfoodmarket.ie)
Good Food Ireland (www.goodfoodireland.ie)
Grá Chocolates (www.grachocolates.com)
Grow It Yourself (GIY) (www.giy.ie)
Guaranteed Irish (www.guaranteedirish.ie)
Holland & Barrett (www.hollandandbarrett.com)
Independent Irish Health Foods Ltd (www.iihealthfoods.com)
IndieFude (www.indiefude.com)
Irish Casing Company Ltd (www.irishcasings.com)
Irish Countrywomen's Association (www.ica.ie)
Irish Farmers Association (www.ifa.ie)
Irish Food Writers Guild (www.irishfoodwritersguild.ie)
Irish Fowl (www.irishfowl.com)
Irish Organic Farmers & Growers Association (www.iofga.org)
Irish Organisation Market & Street Traders (IOMST) (www.iomst.ie)
Irish Village Markets Ltd (www.irishvillagemarkets.ie)
London Farmers' Markets (www.lfm.org.uk)
Love Irish Food (www.loveirishfood.ie)
MacEoin Poultry Supplies Ltd (www.maceoinltd.com)
Markets Alive Support Team Ltd (MAST) (www.mast.ie)
Maxol Homegrown (www.maxol.ie/homegrown/)
Moy Valley Resources IRD (www.moyvalley.ie)
Musgrave Food Services/Musgrave Retailer Services
    (www.musgravemarketplace.co.uk/foodservice/)
Namecheck (www.namecheck.com)
National Ploughing Association – National Ploughing Championships
    (www.npa.ie)
Neighbourfood (www.neighbourfood.ie)
Organic Trust Ltd (www.organic-trust.org)
Quickcrop (www.quickcrop.ie)
Raw Milk Ireland (www.rawmilkireland.com)
Small Firms Association (www.sfa.ie)
Smallholding Ireland (www.smallholding.ie)
Society of Dairy Technology (www.sdt.org)
SuperValu (www.supervalu.ie)
Taste of Scotland (www.taste-of-scotland.com)
Taste the View (www.tastetheview.ie)
Tesco (www.tesco.ie or www.tesco.com)
Too Good To Go (www.toogoodtogo.com/en-ie/)
Well Spent Grain/Born Again Bites (www.well-spent-grain.com)
Wholefoods Wholesale Ltd (www.wholefoods.ie)

# 18

# DIRECTORY

Abernethy Butter (www.abernethybutter.com)

About Hygiene Ltd (www.about-hygiene.com)

Academy of Cheese (UK) (www.academyofcheese.org)

Achill Island Sea Salt (www.achillislandseasalt.ie)

*Action Plan* (www.alphaomega.ie/shop/)

Advanced Food & Drink Manufacturing Network (NI) (www.www.afdmnetwork.com)

AFBI, Belfast (www.afbini.gov.uk/contacts/sensory-evaluation-unit/)

Agriculture & Horticulture Development Board (www.ahdb.org.uk)

Aldi (www.aldi.ie)

Aldi/Grow with Aldi (UK) (www.aldi.co.uk/corporate/suppliers/)

Aldi/Grow with Aldi (www.aldi.ie/grow/)

Aldi/National Brown Bread baking competition (www.aldi.ie/brown-bread-competition/)

Aldi & Channel 4/Aldi's Next Big Thing (www.aldi.co.uk/next-big-thing/)

Alfred & Co. (www.alfredandco.com)

ALPMA GB Ltd (www.alpma.co.uk)

ALS Testing (UK) (www.als-testing.co.uk/services/consultancy-training/)

Amárach Research (www.amarach.com/seven-reasons/food-sensory-panels.html)

Amazon (business.amazon.co.uk, sell.amazon.co.uk, www.sell.amazon.de/en/, www.amazon.ie)

Andrews Food Ingredients (www.andrewsingredients.co.uk)

Animal & Plant Health Agency (UK) (www.apha.gov.uk, www.gov.uk/government/organisations/animal-and-plant-health-agency/)

Applegreen (www.applegreenstores.com)

Aramark (www.aramark.ie)

Ardkeen Stores (www.ardkeen.com)

Arran's Food Journey (www.arransfoodjourney.com)

ASDA / Becoming a supplier (www.rangeme.com/asda/, www.asdasupplier.com/becoming-a-supplier/)

Ashwood Trade Products (UK) (www.ashwood.biz)

Associated Craft Butchers of Ireland/National Butchery Apprenticeship (www.craftbutchers.ie)

Association of Show and Agricultural Organisations (www.asao.co.uk/events/)

ATU, Galway (www.atu.ie)

Avoca (www.avoca.com)

Ayreshire Food an' a' That (www.ayrshirefood.org)

B-Corp (www.bcorporation.net/en-us/)

B-Lab Europe/B-Lab UK (www.bcorporation.eu)

Bakery Bits Ltd (www.bakerybits.co.uk)

Ballykilcavan Brewery (www.ballykilcavan.com/tours.html)

Ballymaloe Cookery School (www.ballymaloecookeryschool.ie)

Bee Farmers Association (www.beefarmers.co.uk)

Bia Sol (www.biasol.ie)

Big Barn (www.bigbarn.co.uk)

BIS Research (www.bisresearch.com)

Black Mountain Smokery (www.smokedfoods.co.uk)

*Blas na hÉireann*/National Irish Food Awards (www.irishfoodawards.com)

Blenders (www.blenders.ie)

Booths/Becoming a supplier (supply.booths.co.uk)

Bord Bia (www.bordbia.ie, www.bordbia.ie/industry/smallbusiness/, www.bordbia.ie/industry/exportassistance/)

Bord Bia Bloom (www.bordbiabloom.com)

*Bord Bia Foodservice Directory* (www.bordbia.info/Foodservices-2023/)

Bord Bia Origin Green (www.origingreen.ie)

Bord Bia Quality Assurance Scheme (www.bordbia.ie/farmersgrowers/get-involved/become-quality-assured/)

Borough Market (www.boroughmarket.org.uk)

Boyne Valley Flavours (www.boynevalleyflavours.ie)

Brandshapers Ltd. (www.brandshapers.ie)

*Bread Science* / Emily Buehler

Brennan Group (www.brennan-group.com)

Bristol Food Producers (www.bristolfoodproducers.uk)

British Cheese Awards (www.britishcheeseawards.com)

British Retail Consortium (www.brcgs.com)

British Retail Consortium/Elearning (www.brcgs.com/training/e-learning/)

Broughgammon Farm (NI) (www.broughgammon.com/events/)

Budgens (www.budgens.co.uk/about-us/)

Costcutter/*Bia Éireannach* programme (www.costcutter.ie)
Cotswold Taste (www.cotswoldtaste.co.uk)
County Dublin Beekeepers' Association (www.dublinbees.org)
Craft Food Traders (www.craftfoodtraders.ie)
Created in Cavan (www.createdincavan.ie)
Croagh Patrick Seafoods (www.croaghpatrickseafoods.ie/tours/)
Curran Foods (www.curranfoods.ie)
*Dairy Microbiology* / RK Robinson (1981)
Dairy UK (www.dairyuk.org)
DairyCo (Ukraine) (www.dairyco.com.ua)
Dairyglen (www.dairyglen.ie)
Deliciously Yorkshire (www.deliciouslyorkshire.co.uk)
Department for Business & Trade/UK Export Academy (www.great.gov.uk)
Department of Agriculture, Environment & Rural Affairs (DAERA) (NI)
    (www.daera-ni.gov.uk/grants-and-funding/food-grants/,
    (www.daera-ni.gov.uk/topics/ruraldevelopment/ruraldevelopment-
    programme/)
Department of Agriculture, Food & the Marine
    (www.gov.ie/en/organisation/department-of-agriculture-food-and-
    the-marine/, www.agriculture.gov.ie)
Department of Enterprise, Trade & Employment
    (https://supportingsmes.gov.ie)
DoneDeal (www.donedeal.ie)
Donegal Food Coast (www.donegalfoodcoast.ie/map/)
Dorset Food & Drink (www.dorsetfoodanddrink.org)
Drop Chef (www.dropchef.com)
Dublin Food Chain (www.dublinfoodchain.ie)
Dunnes Stores/Becoming a Simply Better producer
    (www.dunnesstoresgrocery.com/sm/delivery/rsid/258/
    simplybetter-producers/)
East Lothian Food & Drink (www.scotlandsfooddrinkcounty.com)
Easy Equipment (www.easyequipment.ie)
Eat & Visit SW Scotland (www.facebook.com/eatswscotland/)
Eat Sleep Live Herefordshire (www.eatsleepliveherefordshire.co.uk)
Ebay (www.ebay.ie)
EIT Food (www.eitfood.eu)
ENSO Initiatives (www.ensoimpact.com)
Enterprise Causeway (www.enterprisecauseway.co.uk)
Enterprise Ireland (www.enterprise-ireland.com/en/)
Enterprise Ireland/Innovation Vouchers (www.enterprise-
    ireland.com/en/supports/innovation-voucher/)
Enterprise NI (www.enterpriseni.com/councils/)
Enterprise Revolution (Tees Valley) (www.enterpriserevolution.co.uk)

Environmental Health Association of Ireland (www.ehai.ie,
    www.ehai.ie/courses/)
Environmental Protection Agency/*Air Quality Regulations* (www.epa.ie)
Environmental Protection Agency/*Food Waste Charter*
    (www.foodwastecharter.ie)
Environmental Protection Agency/Stop Food Waste (www.epa.ie)
Eolas International (www.eolasinternational.com)
Euro-toques (www.euro-toques.ie)
Euro-toques Food Awards (www.euro-toques.ie/food-awards-2/)
European Private Label Awards (www.privatelabelawards.com)
*Facebook Marketing* / Louise McDonnell / The Liffey Press
Fáilte Ireland (www.failteireland.ie/foodtourism.aspx)
FareShare (www.fareshare.org.uk)
Farmers' and Country markets (NI) (www.discovernorthernireland.com)
Farmers' and Country markets (Scotland)
    (www.scotlandwelcomesyou.com/scottish-farmers-markets/)
Farmers' and Country markets (Wales)
    (www.welshcountry.co.uk/farmersmarkets-in-wales/)
Farmfoods UK (www.farmfoods.co.uk/become-a-supplier/)
*Farmhouse Cheese* (www.bordbia.ie/farmhouse-cheese/)
*Farmhouse Cheese Factsheet* (www.teagasc.ie)
Federation of Irish Beekeepers' Associations (www.irishbeekeeping.ie)
*Flying Off the Shelves: The Food Entrepreneur's Guide to Selling* / Tessa Stuart
Food & Drink Expo (www.foodanddrinkexpo.co.uk)
Food & Drink Exporters Association (UK) (www.ukfdea.com)
Food & Drink Federation (www.fdf.org.uk)
Food & Drink Forum (www.foodanddrinkforum.co.uk)
Food & Drink North East (www.fadne.org)
Food & Drink Wales (www.food-drink.wales)
Food & Drink Wales Cluster Network (www.businesswales.gov.wales/
    foodanddrink/growing-your-business/clusters/)
Food Business Incubation Centre (www.cafre.ac.uk)
Food business registration (UK) (www.gov.uk/food-business-registration/)
Food Drink Devon (www.fooddrinkdevon.co.uk)
Food festivals (UK) (www.visitbritain.com/en/things-to-do/british-
    food-festivals-you-dont-want-miss/)
Food Flow Advisors (www.foodflow.ie)
Food from England (www.foodfromengland.co.uk)
Food Hygiene Rating scheme (UK) (https://ratings.food.gov.uk)
*Food Hygiene: A Guide for Businesses* (www.food.gov.uk)
Food Industry Training Unit (www.ucc.ie/fitu/)
Food Innovation Wales (www.foodinnovation.wales)

Food labelling (UK) (www.gov.uk/foodlabelling-and-packaging/food-labelling-what-you-must-show/)

Food NI (www.nigoodfood.com)

Food Safety Authority of Ireland (www.fsai.ie)

Food Safety Authority of Ireland/Competent Authorities (www.fsai.ie/business-advice/starting-a-food-business/competent-authorities/)

Food Safety Authority of Ireland/Training (www.fsai.ie/business-advice/running-a-food-business/training-and-online-learning/elearning/)

*Food Safety Workbook for Farmhouse Cheesemakers* (www.fsai.ie/publications/)

Food Standards Agency (NI, England and Wales) (www.food.gov.uk)

Food Standards Agency/Allergen labelling (www.food.gov.uk/business-guidance/allergen-guidance-for-food-businesses/)

Food Standards Agency/Elearning (www.food.gov.uk/businessguidance/online-food-safety-training/)

Food Standards Agency/Food Business Support Hub (www.food.gov.uk/here-to-help)

Food Standards Agency/Food Labelling elearning (www.labellingtraining.food.gov.uk)

Food Standards Agency/Inspections (www.food.gov.uk/businessindustry/hygieneratings/food-law-inspections/)

Food Standards Agency/NI (www.food.gov.uk/northern-ireland/)

Food Standards Agency/Nutrition labelling (www.food.gov.uk/business-guidance/nutrition-labelling/)

Food Standards Agency/Registration of new food business (register.food.gov.uk/new/, www.gov.uk/food-business-registration)

Food Standards Agency/Regulations (www.food.gov.uk/about-us/keyregulations/)

Food Standards Agency/Start-up Checklist (www.food.gov.uk/business-industry/startingup/)

Food Standards Agency/Starting in business (www.food.gov.uk/business-guidance/getting-ready-to-start-your-food-business/, www.food.gov.uk/businessindustry/startingup/, www.food.gov.uk/here-to-help/)

Food Standards Scotland (www.foodstandards.gov.scot)

Food Standards Scotland/Brexit (www.foodstandards.gov.scot/business-and-industry/eu-exit/)

Food Standards Scotland/Elearning (www.foodstandards.gov.scot/business-and-industry/industry-specific-advice/manufacturers/)

Food Standards Scotland/New businesses (www.foodstandards.gov.scot/business-and-industry/advice-for-new-businesses/)

M's Bakery (www.msbakery.co.uk)
MacEoin Poultry Supplies Ltd (www.maceoinltd.com)
Made in Derbyshire (www.madeinderbyshire.org)
Made in Northamptonshire (www.madeinnorthamptonshire.org)
*Manufacturing Yogurt & Fermented Milks* / RC Chandan / Wiley-Blackwell
Marine Scotland (www.marine.gov.scot)
Markets Alive Support Team (www.mast.ie)
Martin Food Equipment (www.martinfoodequip.com)
Maxol/Homegrown at Maxol (www.maxol.ie/homegrown/)
Mayo Food & Drink (www.mayofood.ie/Food Coast Donegal/)
McCambridge's (www.mccambridges.com)
McDonnell's Ltd (www.mcdonnells.ie)
McGrath Bakery Services Ltd (www.mcgrathbakeryservices.com)
McKee's Country Store (www.mckeesproduce.com)
Mescan Brewery (www.mescanbrewery.com)
*Microbiology & Technology of Fermented Foods* (2006) / RW Hutkins
MicroFinance Ireland (www.microfinanceireland.ie)
Midlands Ireland (www.midlandsireland.ie/business/food-and-drink-
    cluster/)
Millar Meats (www.facebook.com/people/Millar-Meats-
    Irvinestown/100051164774815/)
Mindful Chef (www.mindfulchef.com)
MMR Consumer Research (UK) (www.mmr-research.com)
Mobilers Insurance Services (www.mobilers.co.uk)
Moorlands Cheesemakers (www.cheesemaking.co.uk)
Moran's Megajam (www.moransmegajam.ie)
Morrisons/Growing British Brands and Local Foodmakers
    (www.morrisons-corporate.com/suppliers/supplying-morrisons/)
Moy Valley Resources IRD (www.moyvalley.ie)
Musgrave Food Services/Musgrave Retailer Services
    (www.musgravemarketplace.co.uk/foodservice/)
Musgrave Group/SuperValu and Centra (www.musgravegroup.com)
Musgrave Marketplace (www.musgravemarketplace.ie)
My Caboose Store (www.mycaboosestore.ie)
NameCheck (www.namecheck.com)
Natasha's Law (UK) (www.safefood.net/allergens/natashas-law/)
National Association of Cider Makers (www.cideruk.com)
National Dairy Council (www.ndc.ie)
National Enterprise Network (www.nationalenterprisenetwork.org)
National Organic Training Skillnet (www.nots.ie)
National Ploughing Association/National Ploughing Championships
    (www.npa.ie)
Natural Food Expo (www.naturalfoodexpo.co.uk)

Neal's Yard Dairy (www.nealsyarddairy.co.uk)
NeighbourFood (www.neighbourfood.ie, www.neighbourfood.co.uk)
New Food Business Registration (UK) (www.gov.uk/food-business-
    registration/)
New Frontiers programme (www.newfrontiers.ie)
NI Business Info (www.nibusinessinfo.co.uk,
    www.nibusinessinfo.co.uk/business-support/)
NI Good Food/Taste of Ulster (www.nigoodfood.com)
Nisa (www.nisalocally.co.uk)
Nisbets (www.nisbets.ie)
Nobó (www.nobo.ie)
North East Scotland Food & Drink Awards
    (www.nesfoodanddrinkawards.co.uk)
Northern Ireland Food & Drink (www.nifda.co.uk)
Northern Ireland Food & Drink Association Awards
    (www.nifda.co.uk/awards/)
Northern Ireland Regional Food Programme (www.daera-
    ni.gov.uk/articles/northern-ireland-regionalfood-programme/)
Ocado/Becoming a supplier (www.supplyocado.com)
Ocado Retail (www.ocadoretail.com)
Ochil Foods (www.ochilfoods.co.uk)
Odaois Foods (www.odaois-foods.com)
Old Butter Roads (www.oldbutterroads.ie)
Olly's Farm (www.ollysfarm.ie)
Open Food Network (www.openfoodnetwork.org.uk)
Organic Labelling (UK) (www.gov.uk/guidance/organic-food-labelling-
    rules/)
Organic Trust Ltd (www.organic-trust.org)
Oseyo (www.oseyo.co.uk)
*Packaging Suppliers* (www.alphaomega.ie)
*Packed: The Food Entrepreneur's Guide: How to Get Noticed & How to Be
    Loved* / Tessa Stuart
Patents Office (www.gov.uk/browse/business/intellectual-property/,
    www.gov.uk/government/organisations/intellectual-property-office/)
Patents Office (www.patentsoffice.ie)
Planet Organic (www.planetorganic.com)
*Practical Poultry* magazine (www.practicalpoultry.co.uk)
Premier (www.premier-stores.co.uk)
Produce & Provide (www.produceandprovide.co.uk)
Produced in Kent (www.producedinkent.co.uk)
ProQ Smokers (www.proqsmokers.co.uk)
Protected Geographical Indicator (UK) (www.gov.uk/guidance/protect-
    a-geographical-food-or-drink-name-in-the-uk/)

Proudfoot Group (www.proudfootsupermarkets.com/become-a-supplier/)
Quality Food Awards (UK) (uk.qualityfoodawards.com)
Quickcrop (www.quickcrop.ie)
Rademaker BV (Netherlands) (www.rademaker.com)
Range Me (www.rangeme.com)
Raw Milk Ireland (www.rawmilkireland.com)
Raw Milk Producers Association (www.rawmilkproducers.co.uk)
Red Tractor (www.redtractor.org.uk)
Regan Organic Farm (www.reganorganicfarm.ie)
REPAK (www.repak.ie)
Research & Innovation/Innovate UK (www.ukri.org)
Retail Industry Awards (UK) (www.retailindustryawards.com)
Robot Coupe (www.robotcoupe.co.uk)
Rockfield Dairy/Velvet Cloud (www.velvetcloud.ie)
Rora Dairy (www.roradairy.co.uk)
Royal Highland Show (www.royalhighlandshow.org)
RSS Ltd (www.rsshereford.co.uk)
Rural Development Companies/Irish Local Development Network
    (www.ildn.ie/themes/urban-and-rural-development/)
Rural Development Partnerships (LEADER companies)
    (www.nationalruralnetwork.ie, www.leaderprogramme.org.uk)
Rural Development Programmes (England) (www.gov.uk/rural-
    development-programme-for-england/)
Rural Development Programmes (NI) (www.daera-ni.gov.uk/
    topics/rural-development/rural-development-programme/)
Rural Ngage (bbf.uk.com/rural-ngage)
Rustic Boowa (instagram.com/rustic_boowa)
*Safe Catering Pack* (www.fsai.ie)
*safe*food (www.safefood.eu)
*safe*food/Food Hygiene Training (www.safefood.net/safefood-for-
    business/)
Sainsbury's/Becoming a supplier
    (www.about.sainsburys.co.uk/suppliers/becoming-a-supplier/)
SALSA (www.salsafood.co.uk,
    www.salsafood.co.uk/shared/index.php?p=17/)
School of Artisan Food (UK) (www.schoolofartisanfood.org)
Scobie & Junor (Dublin) Ltd (www.scobiesdirect.com)
Scobie Bakery (www.scobiebakery.com)
Scotland Food & Drink (www.foodanddrink.scot)
Scotland Food & Drink/Showcasing Scotland (www.foodanddrink.scot)
Scotland Food & Drink Excellence Awards
    (www.excellenceawards.foodanddrink.scot)

Scottish Farmers' Markets (www.scotlandwelcomesyou.com/scottish-farmers-markets/)

Scottish Funding Council (www.sfc.ac.uk)

Scottish Rural Development Programme (www.ruralpayments.org/topics/all-schemes/food-processing-marketing-and-co-operation/)

Scúp Gelato (www.scupgelato.com)

Sea Fisheries Protection Authority (www.sfpa.ie)

Seafish (UK) (www.seafish.org)

Seafood Scotland (www.seafoodscotland.org)

Selfridge's Food Hall/Becoming a supplier (foodbuyers@selfridges.co.uk)

*Selling at a Scottish Farmers' Market – The First Steps* Scottish Farmers' Markets/Food Standards Agency (www.scotlandwelcomesyou.com/scottish-farmers-markets/, www.food.gov.uk)

SenseLab (UK) (www.sense-lab.co.uk/sensory-testing-facility/)

Shell's Café (www.shellscafe.com)

Sheridan's Cheesemongers (www.sheridanscheesemongers.com)

*Shows and Exhibitions* (www.alphaomega.ie)

Shropshire Food & Drink (www.shropshirefoodanddrink.co.uk)

Siopio (www.siop.io)

Skillnet Ireland (www.skillnetireland.ie)

Sligo Food Trail (www.sligofoodtrail.ie/food-experiences/, www.sligofoodtrail.ie/producers/)

Sligo Oyster Experience (www.sligooysterexperience.ie)

Slow Food (www.slowfood.org.uk)

Slow Food Ireland (www.slowfoodireland.com)

Slow Food NI (www.slowfood.org.uk/slow-food-northernireland/)

Slow Food Scotland (www.slowfoodscotland.com)

Small Business (www.smallbusiness.co.uk)

Small Firms Association (www.sfa.ie)

*Small Scale Production of Fruit Preserves* (www.teagasc.ie)

Smallholding Ireland (www.smallholding.ie)

*Smoked Fish* (www.sfpa.ie)

Smokin' Soul (www.smokinsoul.ie/butchery/)

Society of Dairy Technology (www.sdt.org)

Sodexo (ie.sodexo.com)

SPAR/International Challenger Brand Programme (www.sparinternational.com/suppliers/)

Specialist Cheesemakers Association (www.specialistcheesemakers.co.uk)

Speciality Food Fair (www.specialityandfinefoodfairs.co.uk)

SRL Pharma (www.srlpharmasenses.com/services/)

St. George's Market, Belfast (www.belfastcity.gov.uk/stgeorgesmarket/)

Start & Grow (www.startandgrowuk.org)

*Starting a Business in Ireland* (2023, 8e) / Brian O'Kane / Oak Tree Press (www.successstore.com)

*Starting Your Own Business: A Workbook* (2024, 5e) / Ron Immink & Brian O'Kane / Oak Tree Press (www.successstore.com)

Stop Food Waste (www.stopfoodwaste.ie)

Stratton Sales & Service (USA) (www.strattonsales.com)

Street Food (www.europeanstreetfood.com/2023-awards/)

SuperValu (www.supervalu.ie)

Supplier Development Programme (Scotland) (www.sdpscotland.co.uk/about/)

SupportingSMEs (https://supportingsmes.gov.ie)

Sussex Food & Drink (www.sussexfoodanddrink.org)

Sussex Vineyards (www.sussexmodern.org.uk/wine/)

Sustainable Energy Authority of Ireland (www.seai.ie/business-and-public-sector/business-grants-and-supports/)

Synergy Flavours (UK) (www.uk.synergytaste.com)

Sysco (www.syscoireland.com)

Taste 4 Success Skillnet (www.taste4success.ie)

Taste Causeway (www.tastecauseway.com)

Taste Cheshire (www.tastecheshire.com)

Taste Cork (www.tastecork.ie, www.tastecork.ie/explore-cork/tastetours/craft-beer-brewery-distillery-tours/)

Taste Kerry (www.tastekerry.ie)

Taste Leitrim (www.tasteleitrim.com)

Taste of Scotland (www.taste-of-scotland.com)

Taste of the West (www.tasteofthewest.co.uk)

Taste the View (www.tastetheview.ie)

Taste Waterford (www.tastewaterford.ie)

Teagasc (www.teagasc.ie)

TEDCO (www.tedco.org)

Tesco (www.tesco.ie, www.tesco.com)

Tesco/Becoming a supplier (www.tescoplc.com/contacts/suppliers/, www.tescoplc.com/innovation/innovationcontact/)

Thanks Plants (www.thanksplants.co)

*The Composition of Foods* / McCance & Widdowson / Royal Society of Chemistry

The Food Safety Company (www.thefoodsafetycompany.ie)

The Grill Shack (www.thegrillshack.ie)

The Ice Cream Alliance (UK) (www.ice-cream.org)

*The Irish Foodservice Market Directory* (Bord Bia)

The Organic Centre (www.theorganiccentre.ie)

The Research Suite (sites.google.com/view/theresearchsuite/)

*The Sausage Book* / Paul Peacock / Kitchen Newbie

The Shed Distillery (www.thesheddistillery.com)
The Traditional Cheese Company (www.traditionalcheese.ie)
*The Village Market Handbook* (www.irishvillagemarkets.ie, www.fsai.ie)
The Yorkshire Pantry (www.theyorkshirepantry.com)
TheFoodMarket.com (www.thefoodmarket.com)
Thornhill Duck (www.thornhillduck.com)
Tipperary Food Producers (www.tipperaryfoodproducers.ie)
Too Good To Go (www.toogoodtogo.com/en-ie/)
*Top Ten Tips for Meeting the Buyer* (www.alphaomega.ie)
Total Produce (www.totalproduce.com)
TU Dublin (www.tudublin.ie)
TUS, Limerick (www.lit.ie)
UCC (www.ucc.ie)
UCD (www.ucd.ie)
Údarás na Gaeltachta (www.udaras.ie)
UK Exporting to the EU (www.gov.uk/government/collections/the-windsor-
    framework-further-detail-and-publications/, www.gov.uk/export-goods/)
UK importing from EU (including Ireland) into the UK
    (www.gov.ie/en/publication/668a0-uk-import-controls-2023-the-
    border-target-operating-model-tom/)
UK Innovation Hub/Innovation Vouchers
    (www.ukinnovationhub.ukri.org/offerings/innovation-vouchers/)
Ulster Beekeepers Association (www.ubka.org)
Ulster University (www.ulster.ac.uk)
United Nations Sustainable Development Goals (www.sdgs.un.org/goals/)
*Voluntary Code of Good Practice for Farmers' Markets* (www.bordbia.ie)
Wales Food & Drink Awards (www.foodanddrinkawards.wales)
Well Spent Grain (www.well-spent-grain.com)
Welsh Food & Drink (www.welshfoodanddrink.wales)
Wexford Food Family (www.wexfordfoodfamily.com)
Whole Foods Market (www.wholefoodsmarket.co.uk)
Wholefoods Wholesale Ltd (www.wholefoods.ie)
Wicklow Naturally (www.wicklownaturally.ie)
Wirral Sensory Services (UK) (www.wssintl.com)
World Bread Awards (www.worldbreadawards.com)
World Cheese Awards (www.gff.co.uk/for-producers/worldcheese-
    awards/)
World Drinks Awards (www.worlddrinksawards.com)
World Steak Challenge (www.worldsteakchallenge.com)
WRAP (www.wrap.org.uk)

# ABOUT THE AUTHOR

**OONAGH MONAHAN** has worked in, for and with the food industry for over 25 years, doing everything from waitressing, dishwashing and working in the fast food industry, to food technologist and quality manager in the poultry and bakery sectors, on to academia and finally food business consultancy. She holds a Bachelor of Science from the University of Galway, a Post-Graduate Diploma in Food Science and Technology from TU Dublin and a Masters of Engineering Science degree by research thesis from the Department of Agricultural & Food Engineering at UCD. For this research, Oonagh won a scholarship sponsored by H.J. Heinz to study salad cream in great detail! In addition, Oonagh has a Post Graduate Diploma in Business & Management from the William J. Clinton Leadership Institute at Queen's University Belfast. Oonagh is also a Fellow of the Institute of Food Science and Technology (UK), a Fellow of the Institute of Food Science & Technology of Ireland and a Chartered Scientist (Science Council UK).

Her experience includes roles as Food Technologist and Quality Control Manager with Manor Bakeries Ltd (Mr. Kipling Cakes) in England and Quality Assurance Manager with Kerry Foods (Grove Turkeys) in Co. Monaghan. Oonagh subsequently took a position as General Manager of the Food Technology Centre at St. Angela's College, Sligo (now part of Atlantic Technological University), where she was responsible for business development and growth of the centre, as well as forming and managing collaborative food innovation projects between academia and client food companies. Oonagh has also lectured in food New Product Development and in EU and Irish Food legislation.

In January 2008, Oonagh set up Alpha Omega Consultants, where she uses her extensive experience to devise, deliver, facilitate and manage support programmes for the food, FoodTech and AgTech sectors, as well as providing mentoring and consultancy services in Ireland and across Europe. She has been a mentor with *Blas na hÉireann* (the Irish Food Awards), Enterprise Ireland, several Local Enterprise Offices and Rural Development Companies for both new and established food producers. She also works as a Coach/Mentor with EIT Food (www.eitfood.eu). In addition, Oonagh carries out feasibility studies and develops and implements county food and drink strategies.

Oonagh has delivered Start Your Own Food Business courses across the country, including the Bord Bia/SuperValu Food Academy and Food Starter programmes. She was a founder of the Harvest Feast Food Festival in Leitrim, was involved with the So Sligo Food Festival and was a founder of the Sligo Food Trail. Oonagh has had the very difficult task of being a judge for several Irish and international food and hospitality awards competitions, including *YesChef!*, the Irish Quality Food & Drink Awards (irish.qualityfoodawards.com), and the World Steak challenge – it's not easy!

Oonagh is a keen home cook and has attended several cookery schools, including Neven Maguire's and Ballymaloe. She has a real interest in the preparation, presentation and service of good food, using quality ingredients, local and seasonal where possible, whether fine dining, gastro pub or at home. However, she's not precious about it and recognises the needs of the industry and is pragmatic in her approach. Oonagh always tries to educate consumers, to help them understand labels and differentiate between scientific facts and the nonsense that is too often spouted by self-styled experts, especially on-line.

She has travelled extensively internationally to the UK, France, the Netherlands, Italy, Spain, Portugal, Croatia, Hungary, Bulgaria and the Czech Republic, the USA, Canada, Malaysia and Singapore, as well as extensive travelling throughout the island of Ireland, buying and trying new foods and meeting producers. Places to eat while on the road or on holiday take top priority!

You can follow Oonagh on Twitter and Instagram @oonagheats and on Facebook (www.facebook.com/Oonagheats/).

For more information and for contact details, see LinkedIn (www.linkedin.com/in/oonaghmonahan/) and the Alpha Omega website (www.alphaomega.ie).

# OAK TREE PRESS

Oak Tree Press is Ireland's leading business book publisher, with an unrivalled reputation for quality titles across business, management, HR, law, marketing, and enterprise topics. Its publications are targeted at busy entrepreneurs and managers – always focussing on the effective communication of business information.

**OAK TREE PRESS**

NSC Campus, Mahon, Cork T12 XY2N
T: + 353 021 230 7021
E: info@oaktreepress.com
W: www.oaktreepress.com / www.SuccessStore.com

www.ingramcontent.com/pod-product-compliance
Lightning Source LLC
Chambersburg PA
CBHW070310200326
41518CB00010B/1959

9 7 8 1 7 8 1 1 9 5 8 6 4